CHRISTMAS 2018

Josy Patrick

THIS IS O[...] [...]ST
IMPORTANT BOOKS YOU WILL
EVER READ.

All My Love & Admiration,

DAD

THE SERMON
M O U N T

ON
THE

THE SERMON MOUNT ON THE THE KEY TO SUCCESS IN LIFE

and

THE LORD'S PRAYER

AN INTERPRETATION

Emmet Fox

HarperOne
An Imprint of HarperCollinsPublishers

HarperOne

HarperCollins books may be purchased for educational, business, or sales promotional use. For information please e-mail the Special Markets Department at SPsales@harpercollins.com.

HarperCollins website: http://www.harpercollins.com

HarperCollins®, 📖 ®, and HarperOne™ are trademarks of HarperCollins Publishers.

Designed by Ralph Fowler

Library of Congress Cataloging-in-Publication Data is available upon request.

ISBN 978–0–06–222156–8

12 13 14 15 16   RRD   10 9 8 7 6 5 4 3 2 1

To my students in

Great Britain and America

who have been the inspiration

and encouragement

behind this book

CONTENTS

PREFACE

This book is the distilled essence of years of Bible and metaphysical study, and of the many lectures I have delivered. It would have been easier to have made it twice its present length. My object, however, is to present the reader with a practical manual of spiritual development, and, with this end in view, I have condensed the subject matter into the smallest compass possible, because, as every student knows, conciseness of expression is of the greatest assistance in mastering any subject.

Do not imagine that you can assimilate all that it contains in one or two readings. It should be gone over again and again until you have thoroughly grasped the utterly new outlook upon life and the absolutely fresh scale of values which the Sermon on the Mount presents to mankind. Only then will you experience the New Birth.

The study of the Bible is not unlike the search for diamonds in South Africa. At first people found a few diamonds in the yellow clay, and they were delighted with their good fortune, even while they supposed that this was to be the full extent of their find.

Then, upon digging deeper, they came upon the blue clay, and, to their amazement, they then found as many precious stones in a day as they had previously found in a year, and what had formerly seemed like wealth faded into insignificance beside the new riches.

In your exploration of Bible Truth, see to it that you do not rest satisfied in the yellow clay of a few spiritual discoveries, but press on to the rich blue clay underneath. The Bible, however, differs from the diamond field in the sublime fact that beneath the blue clay there are more and still more and richer strata, awaiting the touch of spiritual perception—on and on to Infinity.

As you read the Bible, you should constantly affirm that Divine Wisdom is enlightening you. That is the way to get direct inspiration.

I have followed a convenient modern custom among writers of metaphysical books in capitalizing certain words that signify aspects or attributes of God.

THE SERMON ON THE MOUNT

CHAPTER ONE

WHAT DID
JESUS TEACH?

Jesus Christ is easily the most important figure that has ever appeared in the history of mankind. It makes no difference how you may regard him, you will have to concede that. This is true whether you choose to call him God or man; and, if man, whether you choose to consider him as the world's greatest Prophet and Teacher, or merely as a well-intentioned fanatic who came to grief, and failure, and ruin, after a short and stormy public career. However you regard him, the fact will remain that the life and death of Jesus, and the teachings attributed to him have influenced the course of human history more than those of any other man who has ever lived; more than Alexander, or Caesar, or Charlemagne, or Napoleon, or Washington. More people's lives are influenced by his doctrines, or at least by the doctrines attributed to him today; more books are written and read and bought concerning him; more speeches are made (call them sermons) concerning him; than concerning all the other names mentioned put together.

To have been the religious inspiration of the whole European race throughout the two millenniums during which that race has dominated and moulded the destinies of the entire world, culturally and socially, as well as politically, and through the period in which the whole of the earth's surface was finally discovered and occupied, and in its broad outlines shaped by civilization; this alone entitles him to the premier position in world importance.

There can hardly, therefore, be a more important undertaking than to inquire into the question of what Jesus really did stand for.

What did Jesus teach? What did he really wish us to believe and to do? What were the objects that he really had at heart? And how far did he actually succeed in accomplishing these objects in his life and in his death? How far has the religion or movement called Christianity, as it has existed for the last nineteen centuries, really expressed or represented his ideas? How far does the Christianity of today present his message to the world? If he should come back now, what would he say of the self-styled Christian nations in general, and of the Christian churches in particular—of the Anglicans, the Baptists, the Catholics, the Greek Orthodox, the

Methodists, the Presbyterians, the Quakers, the Salvationists, the Seventh Day Adventists, or the Unitarians; to cite them alphabetically? What *did* Jesus teach?

This is the question which I have set myself to answer in this book. I propose to show that the message which Jesus brought has a unique value because it is the Truth, and the only perfect statement of the Truth of the nature of God and of man, and of life, and of the world; and of the relationships which exist between them. And far more than this, we shall find that his teaching is not a mere abstract account of the universe, which would be of very little more than academic interest; but that it constitutes a practical method for the development of the soul and for the shaping of our lives and destinies into the things that we really wish them to be.

Jesus explains to us what the nature of God is, and what our own nature is; tells us the meaning of life and of death; shows us why we make mistakes; why we yield to temptation; why we become sick, and impoverished, and old; and, most important of all, he tells us how all these evils may be overcome, and how we may bring health, happiness, and true prosperity into our lives, and into the lives of others, if they really wish for them, too.

The first thing that we have to realize is a fact of fundamental importance, because it means breaking away from all the ordinary prepossessions of orthodoxy. The plain fact is that Jesus taught no theology whatever. His teaching is entirely spiritual or metaphysical. Historical Christianity, unfortunately, has largely concerned itself with theological and doctrinal questions which, strange to say, have no part whatever in the Gospel teaching. It will startle many good people to learn that all the doctrines and theologies of the churches are human inventions built up by their authors out of their own mentalities, and foisted upon the Bible from the outside; but such is the case. *There is absolutely no system of theology or doctrine to be found in the Bible; it simply is not there.* Worthy people who felt the need of some intellectual explanation of life, and also believed that the Bible was a revelation of God to man, drew the natural conclusion that the one must be within the other; and then, more or less unconsciously, proceeded to manufacture the thing that they wished to find. They did not have the spiritual or metaphysical key. They were not upon what is called the Spiritual Basis, and consequently they sought a purely intellectual or three-dimensional explanation of life—and there can be no such explanation.

The actual explanation of man's life lies in just the fact that he is essentially spiritual and eternal, and that this world, and the life that we know intellectually, is, so to speak, but a cross section of the full truth concerning him and a cross section of anything—from a machine to a horse—never can furnish even a partial explanation of the whole.

Glimpsing one tiny corner of the universe, and that with

only half-opened eyes, and working from an exclusively an-thropocentric and geocentric point of view, men built up absurd and very horrible fables about a limited and man-like God who conducted his universe very much as a rather ignorant and barbarous prince might conduct the affairs of a small Oriental kingdom. All sorts of human weaknesses, such as vanity, fickleness, and spite, were attributed to this being. Then a farfetched and very inconsistent legend was built up concerning original sin, vicarious blood atonement, infinite punishment for finite transgressions; and, in certain cases, an unutterably horrible doctrine of predestination to eternal torment, or eternal bliss, was added. Now, no such theory as this is taught in the Bible. If it were the object of the Bible to teach it, it would be clearly stated in a straight-forward manner in some chapter or other; but it is not.

The "Plan of Salvation" which figured so prominently in the evangelical sermons and divinity books of a past gen-eration is as completely unknown to the Bible as it is to the Koran. There never was any such arrangement in the universe, and the Bible does not teach it at all. What has happened is that certain obscure texts from Genesis, a few phrases taken here and there from Paul's letters, and one or two isolated verses from other parts of the Scriptures, have been taken out and pieced together by divines, to produce the kind of teaching which it seemed to them *ought* to have been found in the Bible. Jesus knows nothing of all this. He is indeed anything but a Pollyanna, as they say, or cheap optimist. He warns us, not once but often, that obstinacy in sin can bring very, very severe punishment in its train, and that a man who parts with the integrity of his soul—even though he gain the whole world—is a tragic fool. But he teaches that we are only punished for—and actually punished by—our own mistakes; and he teaches that every man or woman, no matter how steeped in evil and uncleanness, has always direct access to an all-loving, all-powerful Father-God, who will forgive him, and supply His own strength to him to enable him to find himself again; and unto seventy times seven, if need be.

Jesus has been sadly misunderstood and misrepresented in other directions too. For instance, there is no warrant whatever in his teaching for the setting up of any form of Ecclesiasticism, of any hierarchy of officials or system or ritual. He did not authorize any such thing, and, in fact, the whole tone of his mentality is definitely antiecclesiastical. All through his public life he was at war with the ecclesiastics and other religious officials of his own country. They first hindered, and then persecuted him, with a perfectly sound instinct of self-preservation—they felt instinctively that the Truth, as he taught it, was the beginning of the end for them—and they finally had him put to death. Their pretensions to authority as the representatives of God, he ignored completely;

and for their ritual and their ceremonies he evinced only impatience and contempt.

It seems that human nature is very prone to believe what
it wants to believe, rather than to incur the labor of really
searching the Scriptures with an open mind. Perfectly sincere men, for example, have appointed themselves Christian
leaders, with the most imposing and pretentious titles, and
then clothed themselves in elaborate and gorgeous vest-
ments the better to impress the people, in spite of the fact
that their Master, in the plainest language, strictly charged
his followers that they must do nothing of the kind. "But
be ye not called Rabbi: for one is your master, even Christ;
and all ye are brethren" (*Matt.* 23:8). And he denounced the
Pharisees as hypocrites because "they love the chief seats,"
and "bind heavy burdens, grievous to be borne," with all
sorts of rules and regulations.

Jesus, as we shall discover later on, made a special point
of discouraging the laying of emphasis upon outer observances; and, indeed, upon hard-and-fast rules and regulations of every kind. What he insisted upon was a certain
spirit in one's conduct, and he was careful to teach *principles*
only, knowing that when the spirit is right, details will take
care of themselves; and that, in fact, "the letter killeth, but
the spirit giveth life," as was so obviously seen in the sad
example of the Pharisees. Yet, in spite of this, the history

of orthodox Christianity is largely made up of attempts to enforce all sorts of external observances upon the people. A striking case in illustration of this is the Puritan attempt to enforce the Old Testament Sabbath upon Christians, although the Sabbath law was a purely Hebrew ordinance, and the ferocious penalties involved in neglecting it applied exclusively to the desecration of Saturday; and in spite of the fact that Jesus particularly discouraged superstitious Sabbath observance, saying that the Sabbath was made for man and not man for the Sabbath, and making a point of doing anything that he wanted to do upon that day. He clearly indicates throughout his teaching that the time has come when man must make each and every day a spiritual Sabbath by knowing and doing all things in a spiritual light.

It is obvious that even if the Hebrew Sabbath were binding upon Christians, then, since they do not observe it in keeping Sunday, they will still incur all the consequences of Sabbath breaking.

Many modern Christians do, however, realize that there is no system of theology in the Bible unless one likes to put it there deliberately, and they have practically given up theology altogether; but they still cling to Christianity because they feel intuitively that it is the Truth. There is really no logical justification for their attitude, since they do not possess the Spiritual Key which alone makes the teaching of Jesus intelligible, and so they endeavor to rationalize their attitude in various ways. This is the dilemma of the man who has neither the blind faith of orthodoxy nor the spiritual interpretation of Scientific Christianity to support him. He has not a leg to stand on that does not belong to the old-fashioned Unitarian. If he does not reject miracles altogether, he is at least very uneasy about them. They embarrass him, and he wishes they were not in the Bible at all, and would be glad in his heart to be well rid of them.

A "Life of Jesus" recently published by a well-known clergyman clearly illustrates how false this position is. In this book he concedes that Jesus may have healed some people, or helped them to heal themselves, but he draws the line there. He explains away into nothingness all the other miracles. They were the usual fantastic legends that center about all great historical figures, he thinks. On the lake, for instance, the disciples were thoroughly frightened, until they thought of Jesus, and the thought of him calmed their fears. This was subsequently exaggerated into an absurd tale that he had come to them in person walking upon the water. Another time, it appears, he reformed a sinner, raising him out of a grave of sin, and this was expanded, years and years afterwards, into a ridiculous legend that he had really revived a dead man. Again, Jesus prayed fervently one night, so that he looked most radiantly happy, and Peter, who had fallen asleep, woke up with a start; and years afterwards he told some confused story about believing that he saw Moses there—so much for the Transfiguration. And so forth. And so forth.

Now, one must extend every sympathy to the special pleadings of a man enthralled by the beauty and mystery of the Gospels, but who, in the absence of the Spiritual Key, seems to find his common sense and all the scientific knowledge of mankind flouted by much that these Gospels contain. But this simply will not do. If the miracles did not happen, the rest of the Gospel story loses all real significance. If Jesus did not believe them to be possible, and undertake to perform them—never, it is true, for the sake of display, but still constantly and repeatedly—if he did not believe and teach many things in flat contradiction to eighteenth- and nineteenth-century rationalistic philosophy, then the Gospel message is chaotic, contradictory, and devoid of all significance. We cannot ride away from the dilemma by saying that Jesus was not interested in the current beliefs and superstitions of his time; that he took them more or less for granted passively; because what really interested him was *character*. This is a feeble argument, because character must include both an intelligent and a vital all-round reaction to life. Character must include some definite beliefs and convictions concerning things that really matter.

But the miracles did happen. All the deeds related of Jesus in the four Gospels did happen, and many others too, "the which, if they should be written, every one, I suppose that even the world itself could not contain the books that should be written." Jesus himself justified what people thought to be a strange and wonderful teaching by the works he was able to do; and he went further and said, referring to those who study and practice his teaching: "The works that I do, ye shall do, and greater works."

Now what, after all, is a miracle? Those who deny the possibility of miracles on the ground that the universe is a perfect system of law and order, to the operation of which there can be no exceptions, are perfectly right. But the explanation is that the world of which we are normally aware, and with whose laws alone most people are acquainted, is only a fragment of the whole universe as it really is; and that there is such a thing as appealing from a lower to a higher law— from a lesser to a greater expression. Now the appeal from the lower to the higher law is not really a breach of law, for the possibility of such an appeal is part of the major constitution of the universe, and, therefore, in the sense of a real breach of law, miracles are impossible. Yet, in the sense that all the ordinary rules and limitations of the physical plane can be set aside or overridden by an understanding which has risen above them, miracles, in the colloquial sense of the word, can and do happen.

Let us suppose, for the sake of example, that on a certain Monday, your affairs are in such a condition that, humanly speaking, certain consequences are sure to follow before the end of the week. These may be legal consequences, perhaps of a very unpleasant nature following upon some decision of the courts; or they may be certain physical consequences in the human body. A competent physician may decide that a perilous operation will be absolutely necessary, or he may even feel it his duty to say that there is no chance for the recovery of the patient. Now, if someone can raise his consciousness above the limitations of the physical plane in connection with the matter—and this is only a scientific description of what is commonly called prayer—then the conditions on that plane will change, and, in some utterly unforeseen and normally impossible manner, the legal tragedy will melt away, and to the advantage, be it noted, of all parties to the case; or the patient will be healed instead of having to undergo the operation, or of having to die.

In other words, miracles, in the popular sense of the word, can and do happen as the result of prayer. *Prayer does change things.* Prayer does make things happen quite otherwise than they would have happened had the prayer not been made. It makes no difference at all what sort of difficulty you may be in. It does not matter what the causes may have been that led up to it. Enough prayer will get you out of your difficulty if only you will be persistent enough in your appeal to God.

Prayer, however, is both a science and an art; and it was to the teaching of this science and this art that Jesus devoted the greater part of his ministry. The Gospel miracles happened because Jesus had the spiritual understanding that gave him greater power in prayer than anyone else before or since.

One other attempt to interpret the Gospels must be taken into consideration. Tolstoy endeavored to put forward the Sermon on the Mount as a practical guide to life, taking its precepts literally, at their face value, and ignoring the spiritual interpretation of which he was unaware, and excluding the Plane of Spirit in which he did not believe. Discarding the whole of the Bible except the four Gospels, and discounting all miracles, he made a heroic but futile attempt to combine Christianity and materialism; and, of course, he failed. His real place in history turns out to be not that of the founder of a new religious movement, but that of the man whose practical anarchism, promulgated with all the fire of genius, paved the way for the Bolshevik Revolution, even as Rousseau had cleared the road for the French Revolution.

It is the Spiritual Key that unlocks the mystery of the Bible teaching in general, and of the Gospels in particular. It is the Spiritual Key that explains the miracles and shows that they were performed in order to prove to us that we too can perform miracles, and thereby overcome sin, sickness, and limitation. With this key we can afford to discard verbal inspiration and all superstitious literalism, and yet understand that the Bible really is the most precious and most authentic of all man's possessions.

Externally, the Bible is a collection of inspired documents written by men of all kinds, in all sorts of circumstances, and over hundreds of years of time. The documents, as we have them, are seldom originals, but redactions and compilations of older fragments; and the names of the actual writers are seldom known for certain. This, however, does not affect the spiritual purpose of the Bible in the slightest degree; it is in fact quite immaterial. The book, as we have it, is an inexhaustible reservoir, of Spiritual Truth, compiled under Divine Inspiration, and the actual route by which it reached its present form does not matter. The name of the writer of any particular chapter is really of no more importance than would be the name of his amanuensis, if he employed one. Divine Wisdom is the author; and that is all that concerns us. What is called the Higher Criticism concerns itself exclusively with externals, completely missing the spiritual content of the Scriptures, and from the spiritual point of view is of no importance.

History, biography, lyrical and other poetic forms are various mediums through which the spiritual message is given in the Bible; and, above all, the parable is used to convey spiritual and metaphysical truth. In some cases, what was never intended to be more than a parable was, at one time, taken for literal statement of fact; and this often made the

Bible seem to teach things which are opposed to common sense. The story of Adam and Eve and the Garden of Eden is a case in point. Rightly understood, this is perhaps the most wonderful parable of all; it was never intended by its author to be taken for history, but literal-minded people did so take it, with all sorts of absurd consequences.

The Spiritual Key to the Bible rescues us from all these difficulties, dilemmas, and seeming inconsistencies. It saves us from the false positions of Ritualism, Evangelicalism, and what is called Liberalism alike, because it gives us the Truth. And the Truth turns out to be nothing less than the amazing but undeniable fact that the whole outer world—whether it be the physical body, the common things of life, the winds and the rain, the clouds, the earth itself—is amenable to man's thought, and that he has dominion over it when he knows it. The outer world, far from being the prison of circumstances that it is commonly supposed to be, has actually no character whatsoever of its own, either good or bad. It has only the character that we give to it by our own thinking. It is naturally plastic to our thought, and this is so, whether we know it or not, and whether we wish it or not.

All day long the thoughts that occupy your mind, your Secret Place, as Jesus calls it, are moulding your destiny for good or evil; in fact, the truth is that the whole of our life's experience is but the outer expression of inner thought.

Now we can choose the sort of thoughts that we entertain. It will be a little difficult to break a bad habit of thought,
but it can be done. We can choose how we shall think—in
point of fact, we always do choose—and therefore our lives
are just the result of the kind of thoughts we have chosen to
hold; and therefore they are of our own ordering; and therefore there is perfect justice in the universe. No suffering for
another man's original sin, but the reaping of a harvest that
we ourselves have sown. We have free will, but our free will
lies in our choice of thought.

This is in essence what Jesus taught. It is, as we shall see,
the underlying message of the whole Bible; but it is not expressed with equal clearness throughout. In the earlier por-
tion of the book it shines through but dimly on the whole, as
the light from a heavily shrouded lamp; but, as time goes on,
veil after veil is removed, and the light shines ever stronger
and stronger, until, in the teaching of Jesus Christ, it pours
forth clear and unimpeded. Truth never changes, but what
we have to deal with on this plane is man's apprehension
of the Truth, and, throughout historical time, this has been
steadily and continuously improving. In fact, what we call
progress is but the outer expression corresponding to mankind's continuously improving idea of God.

Jesus Christ summed up this Truth, taught it completely
and thoroughly, and, above all, demonstrated it in his own
person. Most of us now can glimpse intellectually the idea of

what it must mean in its fullness, and much that must inevitably follow from a competent understanding of it. But what we can demonstrate is a very different matter. To accept the Truth is the great first step, but not until we have proved it in doing is it ours. Jesus proved everything that he taught, even to the overcoming of death in what we call the Resurrection. For reasons which I cannot discuss here it happens that every time you overcome a difficulty by prayer, you help the whole of the human race, past, present, and future, in a general way; and you help it to overcome that special kind of difficulty in particular. Jesus, by surmounting every sort of limitation to which mankind is subject, and in particular by overcoming death, performed a work of unique and incalculable value to the race, and is therefore justly entitled the Saviour of the world.

At what he deemed an opportune moment in his public ministry, he decided to sum up the whole teaching in a series of lectures extending probably over several days, and speaking probably two or three times a day. This arrangement has been compared by someone, and not inaptly, to a kind of summer school, as we have such things today.

He took this opportunity to summarize the message, to dot the i's and cross the t's, so to say. A number of those present naturally took notes, and, later on, these notes were edited into what we know as the Sermon on the Mount. The authors of the four Gospels each selected the material for his monograph in accordance with his own purpose; and it is Matthew who gives us the most complete and carefully arranged version of the address. His setting forth of the Sermon on the Mount is an almost perfect codification of the Jesus Christ religion, and I have therefore chosen it as the text for this book. It covers the essentials. It is practical and personal. It is definite, specific, and yet widely illuminating. Once the true meaning of the instructions has been grasped, it is only necessary to begin putting them faithfully into practice to get immediate results. The magnitude and extent of these results will depend solely upon the sincerity and thoroughness with which they are applied. This is a matter which each individual has to settle for himself. "No man can save his brother's soul, or pay his brother's debt." We can and should help one another on special occasions, but in the long run each must learn to do his own work, and "sin" no more, lest a worse thing befall him.

If you really do wish to alter your life, if you really do wish to change yourself—to become a different person altogether in the sight of God and man—if you really do want health and peace of mind, and spiritual development, then Jesus, in his Sermon on the Mount, has clearly shown you how it is to be done. The task is not an easy one, but we know that it can be accomplished, because there are those who have done it—but, the price must be paid, and the price is the actual carrying out of these principles in every corner of your life, and in every daily transaction, whether you wish to or not, and more particularly where you would much rather not.

If you are prepared to pay that price, to break really and truly with the old man, and start upon the creation of the new one, then the study of the great Sermon will indeed be to you the Mountain of Liberation.

CHAPTER TWO

THE BEATITUDES

And seeing the multitudes, he went up into a mountain: and when he was set, his disciples came unto him:

And he opened his mouth, and taught them, saying,

Blessed are the poor in spirit: for theirs is the kingdom of heaven.

Blessed are they that mourn: for they shall be comforted.

Blessed are the meek: for they shall inherit the earth.

Blessed are they which do hunger and thirst after righteousness: for they shall be filled.

Blessed are the merciful: for they shall obtain mercy.

Blessed are the pure in heart: for they shall see God.

Blessed are the peacemakers: for they shall be called the children of God.

Blessed are they which are persecuted for righteousness' sake: for theirs is the kingdom of heaven.

Blessed are ye, when men shall revile you, and persecute you, and shall say all manner of evil against you falsely, for my sake.

Rejoice, and be exceeding glad: for great is your reward in heaven: for so persecuted they the prophets which were before you.

—MATTHEW V

T he Sermon on the Mount opens with the Eight Beatitudes. This, of course, is one of the best-known sections of the Bible. Even people whose knowledge of the Scriptures is confined to half a dozen of the most familiar chapters are sure to know the Beatitudes. They hardly ever understand them, unfortunately, and as a rule look upon them as a counsel of perfection, without any real application to everyday life. But this is only because they lack the Spiritual Key.

The Beatitudes are actually a prose poem in eight verses which is complete in itself, and it constitutes what is practically a general summary of the whole Christian teaching. It is a spiritual, more than a literary synopsis, summarizing the spirit of the teaching rather than the letter. A general summing up, such as this, is highly characteristic of the old Oriental mode of approach to a religious and philosophical teaching, and it naturally recalls the Eight-fold Path of Buddhism, the Ten Commandments of Moses, and other such compact groupings of ideas.

Jesus concerned himself exclusively with the teaching of general principles, and these general principles always had to do with mental states, for he knew that if one's mental states are right, everything else must be right too, whereas, if these are wrong, nothing else can be right. Unlike the other great religious teachers, he gives us no detailed instructions about what we are to do or are not to do; he does not tell us either to eat or to drink, or to refrain from eating or drinking certain things; or to carry out various ritual observances at certain times and seasons. Indeed, the whole current of his teaching is anti-ritualistic, anti-formalist. He had little patience at any time with the Jewish priesthood and its theory of salvation through the Temple observances. "The hour cometh when ye shall neither in this mountain, nor yet at Jerusalem, worship the Father. . . . The hour cometh and now is when the true worshipper shall worship the Father in spirit and in truth; for the Father seeketh such to worship him. God is spirit and they that worship Him must worship Him in spirit and in truth."

The Pharisees, with their appalling code of outward detailed observances, were the only people towards whom he was really intolerant. A conscientious Pharisee of those days—and most of them were extremely conscientious, according to their lights—had an enormous number of outer details to attend to every day before he could feel that he had satisfied the requirements of God. A modern rabbi has estimated the number of such details at not less than six hundred, and as it is obvious that no human being could really carry out this sort of thing in practice, the natural result would be that the victim, conscious of falling far short of the accomplishment of his duties, must necessarily labor under a chronic sense of sin. Now, to believe yourself to be sinful is, for practical purposes, to be sinful, with all the consequences that follow upon that condition. The policy of Jesus contrasts with this in that his object is rather to wean the heart from relying upon outer things at all, either for pleasurable gratification or for spiritual salvation, and to inculcate a new attitude of mind altogether; and this policy is graphically set forth in the Beatitudes.

BLESSED ARE THE POOR IN SPIRIT: FOR THEIRS IS THE KINGDOM OF HEAVEN.

Here, in the very beginning, we have to take into account a point of great practical importance in the study of the Bible, namely, that is written in a peculiar idiom of its own, and that terms and expressions, and sometimes actual words, are used in the Bible in a sense that is distinctly different from that of everyday usage. This is quite apart from the fact, for which we have also to be on the lookout, that certain English words have changed in meaning since the Bible was translated.

The Bible is really a textbook of metaphysics, a manual for the growth of the soul, and it looks at all questions from this point of view. It is impossible to emphasize this point too much. For this reason it takes the broadest view of every subject. It sees all things in their relationship to the human soul, and it uses many common terms in a far wider sense than that given to them by common use. For example, the word "bread" in the Bible means, not merely any kind of physical food, which is the broadest interpretation that is put upon it in general literature, but all things that man requires—all physical things, such as clothing, shelter, money, education, companionship, and so forth; and, above all, it stands for spiritual things such as spiritual perception, spiritual under-standing, and preeminently spiritual realization. "Give us this day our daily bread." "I am the bread of life." "Unless ye eat this bread. . . ."

Another example is the word "prosperity." In the scrip-tural sense, "prosperity," and "prosper," signify a very great deal more than the acquirement of material possessions. They really mean success in prayer. From the point of view of the soul, success in prayer is the only kind of prosperity worth having; and if our prayers are successful, we shall naturally have all the material things that we need. A cer-tain quantity of material goods is essential on this plane, of course, but material wealth is really the least important thing in life, and this the Bible implies by giving the word "prosperous" its true meaning.

To be *poor in spirit* does not in the least mean the thing we call "poor spirited" nowadays. To be *poor in spirit* means to have emptied yourself of all desire to exercise personal self-will, and, what is just as important, to have renounced all preconceived opinions in the wholehearted search for God. It means to be willing to set aside your present habits of thought, your present views and prejudices, your present way of life if necessary; to jettison, in fact, anything and everything that can stand in the way of your finding God.

One of the saddest passages in all literature is the story of the Rich Young Man who missed one of the great opportunities of history, and "turned away sorrowful because he had great possessions." This is really the story of mankind in general. We reject the salvation that Jesus offers us—our chance of finding God—because we "have great possessions"; not in the least because we are very rich in terms of money, for indeed most people are not, but because we have great possessions in the way of preconceived ideas—confidence in our own judgment, and in the ideas with which we happen to be familiar; spiritual pride, born of academic distinction; sentimental or material attachment to institutions and organizations; habits of life that we have no desire to renounce; concern for human respect, or perhaps fear of public ridicule; or a vested interest in worldly honor and distinction. And these possessions keep us chained to the rock of suffering that is our exile from God.

The Rich Young Man is one of the most tragic figures in history; not because he happened to be wealthy, for wealth in itself is neither good nor bad, but because his heart was enslaved by that love of money which Paul tells us is the root of all evil. He could have been a multimillionaire in silver and gold, and, as long as his heart was not set upon it, he would have been just as free as the poorest beggar to enter the Kingdom of Heaven. His trust, however, was in his riches, and this shut the gate.

Why was not the Christ Message received with acclaim by the Ecclesiastics of Jerusalem? Because they had great possessions—possessions of Rabbinical learning, possessions of public honor and importance, authoritative offices as the official teachers of religion—and these possessions they would have had to sacrifice in order to accept the spiritual teaching. The humble and unlearned folk who heard the Master gladly were happy in having no such possessions to tempt them away from the Truth.

Why was it in modern times when the same simple Christ Message of the immanence and availability of God, and of the Inner Light that burns forever in the soul of man, once more made its appearance in the world, it was again, for the most part, among the simple and unlettered that it was gladly received? Why was it not the Bishops, and Deans, and Moderators, and Ministers, and Presbyteries, who gave it to the world? Why was not Oxford, or Cambridge, or Harvard, or Heidelberg, the great broadcasting center for this most important of all knowledge? And, again the answer is—because they had great possessions—great possessions of intellectual and spiritual pride, great possessions of self-satisfaction and cocksureness, great possessions of academic commitment, and of social prestige.

The *poor in spirit* suffer from none of these embarrassments, either because they never had them, or because they have risen above them on the tide of spiritual understanding. They have got rid of the love of money and property, of fear of public opinion, and of the disapproval of relatives or friends. They are no longer overawed by human authority, however august. They are no longer cocksure in their own opinions. They have come to see that their most cherished beliefs may have been and probably were mistaken, and that all their ideas and views of life may be false and in need of recasting. They are ready to start again at the very beginning and learn life anew.

BLESSED ARE THEY THAT MOURN: FOR THEY SHALL BE COMFORTED.

Mourning or sorrow is not in itself a good thing, for the Will of God is that everyone should experience happiness and joyous success. Jesus says: "I am come that they might have life, and that they might have it more abundantly." Nevertheless, trouble and suffering are often extremely useful, because many people will not bother to learn the Truth until driven to do so by sorrow and failure. Sorrow then becomes relatively a good thing. Sooner or later every human being will have to discover the Truth about God, and make his own contact with Him at first hand. He will have to acquire the understanding of Truth, which will set him free, once and for all, from our three-dimensional limitations and their concomitants—sin, sickness, and death. But most people will not undertake the search for God wholeheartedly unless driven thereto by trouble of some kind. There is really no need for man to have trouble, because if he will only seek God first, the trouble need never come. He always has the choice of learning by spiritual unfoldment or of learning by painful experience, and it is his own fault if he makes the latter choice.

As a rule, it is only when health is broken down, and ordinary medical means have failed to afford relief, that people seriously set about gaining that spiritual understanding of the body as the true embodiment of Divine Life that is our only guarantee of overcoming sickness and, ultimately, death. Yet, if people would turn to God and acquire something of this understanding while their health is still good, they need never be sick at all.

Again, it is usually only when people are feeling the pinch of poverty very acutely, that is, when ordinary material sources of supply have dried up, that they turn to God as a last resort and learn the lesson that the Divine Power really is the *Source* of man's supply, and all material agents but the *channels*.

Now this lesson has to be learned and thoroughly realized before man can pass on to any experience higher or wider than the present one. In our Father's House are many mansions, but the key to higher mansions is always the acquiring of complete dominion over the one in which we are. It is therefore a very blessed thing for us that we should be compelled to get right on the supply question at the earliest possible moment. If prosperous people will now, while they are still prosperous, acknowledge God as their true Source, and pray regularly for still more spiritual understanding on this point, they need never suffer poverty or financial trouble at all. At the same time, they must be careful to use their present resources well, not hoarding riches selfishly but recognizing that God is the owner, and that they are only the stewards or trustees for Him. The command of money involves a responsibility which you cannot evade. You must dispense it wisely, or take the consequences.

This general principle applies to every one of our difficulties, not merely physical or financial troubles, but all the other ills to which flesh is heir. Family troubles, quarrels and estrangements, sin and remorse, and all the rest, need never come at all if we will seek first the Kingdom of God and Right Understanding; but if we will not do so, then come they must, and for us this mourning will be a blessing in disguise, for through it we shall be "comforted." And by comfort the Bible means the experience of the Presence of God, which is the end of all mourning.

The orthodox churches have too often taught a crucified Christ finishing on the cross; but the Bible gives us the Risen Christ Triumphant.

BLESSED ARE THE MEEK: FOR THEY SHALL INHERIT THE EARTH.

On the surface, this Beatitude seems to have very little meaning, and what there is seems to be obviously contradicted by the plain facts of everyday life. No sensible person on looking about the world or studying history could sincerely accept this saying at its face value, and most honest Christians have passed it by in practice with a regretful feeling that no doubt that is how things ought to be, but that they certainly are not so in fact.

But this attitude will not do. Sooner or later the soul reaches a point where evasions and sophistries have to be discarded once and for all, and the fact of life faced squarely at whatever cost.

Now, either Jesus meant what he said, or he did not; and either he knew what he was talking about, or he did not. And so, if this saying is not to be taken seriously, we are driven to the position which no Christian will care to accept—either that Jesus was saying what he did not really believe, as unscrupulous people do, or that he was talking nonsense. We have to face up to this situation at the very beginning of our study of this Sermon on the Mount. Either Jesus is to be taken seriously, or he is not to be taken seriously, in which case his teaching should be dropped altogether and people should cease to call themselves Christians. To pay lip service to his name, to say that Christianity is the divinely inspired Truth, to boast of being Christians, and then quietly to evade in practice all the definite implications of his teaching, is hypocrisy and weakness of the most utterly fatal kind. Either Jesus is a reliable guide, or he is not. If he is to be relied upon, then let us pay him the compliment of assuming that he meant what he said, and that he knew best about the art of living. The trouble and sorrow that humanity suffers are really due to the very fact that our mode of life is so opposed to the Truth, that the things that he taught and the things that he said seem to us at first sight to be foolish and wild.

The fact is that when correctly understood, the teaching of Jesus is found to be not only true but exceedingly practicable; indeed it is the most practicable of all doctrines. We find then that he was no sentimental dreamer, no mere dealer in empty platitudes, but the unflinching realist that only a great mystic can be; and the whole essence of his teaching of its practical application is summed up in this text.

This Beatitude is among the half-dozen most important verses in the Bible. When you possess the spiritual meaning of this text you have the Secret of Dominion—the secret of overcoming every kind of difficulty. It is literally the Key of Life. It is the Jesus Christ Message reduced to a single sentence. This gnomic saying is actually the Philosopher's Stone of the Alchemists that turns the base metal of limitation and trouble into the gold of "comfort" or true harmony.

We notice that there are two polar words in the text—"meek" and "earth." They are both used in a special and highly technical sense, and they have to be unveiled before the wonderful meaning that underlies them can be found. First, of all, the word "earth" in the Bible does not mean merely this terrestrial globe. It really means manifestation. Manifestation or expression is the result of a cause. A cause has to be expressed or manifested before we can know anything about it; and, contrariwise, every expression or manifestation has to have a cause. Now you learn in Divine Metaphysics, and particularly in the Sermon on the Mount, that *all causation is mental,* and that your body and all your affairs—your home, your business, all your experience—are but the manifestation of your own mental states. The fact that you are quite unconscious of most of your mental states does not signify; because they are there, nevertheless, in your subconscious mind, notwithstanding the fact that you have now forgotten them, or never were aware of them at all.

In other words, your "earth" means the whole of your outer experience, and to "inherit the earth" means to have dominion over that outer experience; that is to say, to have power to bring your conditions of life into harmony and true success. "All the earth shall be filled with the glory of the Lord." "His soul shall dwell at ease, and His seed (prayers) shall inherit the earth." "The Lord reigneth, let the earth rejoice." So we see that when the Bible talks about the earth—possessing the earth, governing the earth, making the earth glorious, and so forth—it is referring to the conditions of our lives from our bodily health outwards to the farthest point in our affairs. So this text undertakes to tell us how we may possess, or govern, to be masters of our own lives and destinies.

Now let us see how it is to be done. The Beatitude says that dominion, that is, power over the conditions of our lives, is to be obtained in a certain way, and in the most unexpected of all ways—by nothing less than meekness. The fact is, however, that this word "meekness" also is used in a special and technical sense. Its true significance has nothing in common with the meaning it now bears in modern English. Actually, there are few more unpleasant qualities in human nature than the one that is nowadays denoted by the word "meekness." To a modern reader, the "meek" suggests a mean-spirited creature, devoid alike of courage and self-respect, of no use to himself or anyone else, crawling over the face of the earth like a worm, and probably hypocritical and mean as well. It suggests Dickens's fawning Uriah Heep at worst, and one of the same author's downtrodden, broken-spirited moral wrecks at best. But Dickens always holds such characters up for warning or ridicule, and never for emulation. The modern reader, with these connotations of the word in mind, comes to the Sermon on the Mount and rejects the teaching that it gives because, here on the threshold, he is told that dominion is for the meek; and this doctrine he cannot accept.

The true significance of the word "meek" in the Bible is a mental attitude for which there is no other single word available, and it is this mental attitude which is the secret of "prosperity" or success in prayer. It is a combination of open-mindedness, faith in God, and the realization that the Will of God for us is always something joyous and interesting and vital, and much better than anything we could think of for ourselves. This state of mind also includes a perfect willingness to allow this Will of God to come about in whatever way Divine Wisdom considers to be best, rather than in some particular way that we have chosen for ourselves.

This mental attitude, complex in analysis but simple in itself, is the Key to Dominion, or success in demonstration. There is no one word for it in common speech, because the thing does not exist except for those who are upon the Spiritual Basis of the Jesus Christ teaching; but if we desire to *inherit the earth* we must absolutely acquire this "meekness."

Moses, who had such extraordinary success in prayer—
he overcame the old-age belief to the extent of manifest-
ing the physical body of a young man in the prime of life,
when, according to the calendar, he was one hundred and
twenty years old, and then transcended matter altogether,
or, "dematerialized" without dying—was known preeminently for this quality—"as meek as Moses." Moses, we remember, apart from his own personal demonstration, did a
marvelous work for his whole nation, getting it out of Egyptian bondage in the face of incredible difficulties (for the
successful Exodus was the "demonstration" of Moses and a
few advanced souls who were helping him) and influencing
the whole subsequent course of history by his teaching and
his deeds. Moses had an open mind, ready to be taught new
things and new ways of thinking and working. He did not
reject fresh revelation because it was novel and revolutionary, as most of his self-satisfied colleagues in the Egyptian
Hierarchy would have done. He was not, in the beginning at
least, free from serious faults of character, but he was too big
for intellectual or spiritual pride, and therefore he gradually
rose above these defects as the new truth worked in his soul.

Moses thoroughly understood that to conform oneself
rigorously to the Will of God, far from involving the loss of
any good, could only mean a finer and better and more splendid life. He did not, therefore, think of it as self-sacrifice, for
he knew it to be the highest form of self-glorification in the

true and wonderful sense of the word. The self-glorification of the egotist is the mean vanity that leads at last to humiliation. True self-glorification, the glorification that is really glorious, is the glorification of God—"The Father in me, He doeth the works." "I in Thee, and Thou in Me." Moses had a wonderful understanding of the power of the spoken Word to call forth good, which is scientific faith. He was one of the "meekest" men who ever lived, and no one, excepting our Saviour, has *inherited the earth* to a greater degree.

There is a marvelous Oriental saying that "Meekness compels God Himself."

BLESSED ARE THEY WHICH
DO HUNGER AND THIRST
AFTER RIGHTEOUSNESS: FOR
THEY SHALL BE FILLED.

"Righteousness" is another of the great Key Words of the Bible, one of those keys that the reader must have in his possession if he is to get at the true meaning of the book. Like "earth" and "meek" and "comfort," it is a technical term used in a special and definite sense.

Righteousness means, in the Bible, not merely right conduct, but right thinking on all subjects, in every department of life. As we study the Sermon on the Mount, we shall find every clause in it reiterating the great truth that outside things are but the expression (ex-pressed or pressed out) or out-picturing of our inner thoughts and beliefs; that we have dominion or power over our thoughts to think as we will; and thus, indirectly, we make or mar our lives by the way in which we do think. Jesus will constantly tell us in these discourses that we have no direct power over outer things, because these outer things are but consequences, or, if you like, resultant pictures of what goes on in the Secret Place. If it were possible for us to affect externals directly without changing our thought, it would mean that we could think one thing and produce another; and this would be contrary to the Law of the Universe. Indeed, it is just this very notion which is the basic fallacy that lies at the root of all human trouble—all sickness and sin, all strife and poverty, and even death itself.

The great Law of the Universe, however, is just this—that what you think in your mind you will produce in your experience. *As within, so without.* You cannot think one thing and produce another. If you want to control your circumstances for harmony and happiness, you must first control your thoughts for harmony and happiness, and then the outer things will follow. If you want health, you must first think health; and, remember, thinking health does not mean merely thinking a healthy body, important as that is, but it also includes thinking peace and contentment, and good-will to all, for, as we shall see later on in the Sermon, destructive emotion is one of the primary causes of disease. If you want spiritual unfoldment and growth in the knowledge of God, you must think spiritual thoughts—God thoughts—and give your attention, which is your life, to God rather than to limitation.

If you want material prosperity, you must first think prosperity thoughts, and then *make a habit* of doing so, for the thing that keeps most people poor is the sheer habit of poverty thinking. If you want congenial companionship, if you want to be loved, you must first think thoughts of love and good-will. *Like begets like,* is another way of stating the Great Law, which means that as a man soweth in his unseen thoughts, so shall he reap in that which is seen. "All things work together for good to those who love good," and to love good means to occupy oneself with thoughts of good.

When people awaken to a knowledge of these great truths, they naturally try to begin to apply them in their own lives. Realizing at last the vital importance of "righteousness," or the thinking of harmonious thoughts, they, as sensible people, begin immediately to try to put their house in order. The principle involved is perfectly simple, but unfortunately the doing of it is anything but easy. Now, why should this be so? The answer lies in the extraordinary potency of habit; and habits of thinking are at once the most subtle in character and the most difficult to break. It is easy, comparatively speaking, to break a physical habit if one really means business, because action on the physical plane is so much slower and more palpable than on the mental plane. In dealing with habits of thought, however, we cannot, so to say, stand back and take a comparatively detached view, as we can in contemplating our actions. Our thoughts flow across the stage of consciousness in an unbroken stream, and so rapidly that only unceasing vigilance can deal with them. Again, the theatre of one's actions is the area of his immediate presence. I can act only where I am. I may give orders by letter, or telephone; or I may press a button and bring about results at a distance; but still, my action happens where I am, and at the present moment of time. In thought, on the contrary, I can range over the whole area of my life, including all the people with whom I have been or am in any way concerned, and I can soar away into the past or into the future with equal ease. We see, therefore, how much bigger the task of achieving all-around harmonious thinking, or true righteousness, is than appears at first sight.

For this reason many people become discouraged with themselves and indulge in a great deal of self-condemnation because they do not very speedily change the whole current of thought over the whole area of their lives—destroy the old Adam, as Paul says—in a very short time. This, of course, is a capital mistake and, incidentally, self-condemnation being an essentially negative, and therefore unrighteous thought, tends to produce still more trouble, in the old vicious circle. If you are not progressing as fast as you wish to, the remedy is—to be still more careful to hold only harmonious thoughts. Do not dwell upon your mistakes or upon the slowness of your progress, but claim the Presence of God with you, all the more, in the teeth of the discouraging suggestion. Claim Wisdom. Claim Power, or prosperity in prayer. Have a mental stocktaking or a review of your life, and see if you are not still thinking wrongly in some section or other of your mind. Is there some wrong line of conduct that you are still pursuing? Is there somebody whom you have not yet forgiven? Are you indulging in any kind of political, or racial, or religious sectarian hatred or contempt? This is sure to be disguising itself under a cloak of self-righteousness, if it is there. If it is, tear off the cloak, and get rid of the evil thing, for it is poison in your life. Is there some kind of jealousy left in your heart—it may be personal or it may be professional. This odious thing is a good deal more common than would be readily admitted in polite society. If it is there, cut it out at any cost. Are there any sentimental regrets, or purposeless yearnings for the impossible? If so, reflect that, as an immortal being, the Son of God holding spiritual dominion, no good thing is out of your reach, here and now. Waste no more time repining for what is over and done, but make the present and the future a splendid realization of your heart's desire. Is there remorse for mistakes past and gone? Then remember that remorse, as distinct from repentance, is merely a form of spiritual pride. To revel in it, as some people do, is treason to the love and forgiveness of God, who says: "Behold now is the day of salvation." "Behold I make all things new."

In this Beatitude, Jesus tells us not to be discouraged because we do not overcome everything at once, because our progress seems to be slow. If we are not making any progress at all, then we cannot be praying in the right way, and it is for us to find out why, by examining our lives, and by praying for wisdom and guidance. Indeed, we should constantly pray for wisdom and guidance, and for the living action of the Holy Spirit upon us, that the quality of our prayers—our prosperity—may constantly increase. But if we are moving, if things are improving, although not very quickly it may be, we have no need to be discouraged. We need only to work on steadily, and provided we are truly wholehearted in our efforts, provided, that is to say, that we really are *hungering and thirsting for righteousness*, then, at last, we shall surely be filled. It could not happen that a wholehearted search for truth and righteousness, if persevered in, should not be crowned with success. God is not mocked, nor does He mock His children.

BLESSED ARE THE MERCIFUL:
FOR THEY SHALL OBTAIN MERCY.

This is a brief summary of the Law of Life which Jesus develops more fully later in the Sermon (*Matt.* 7: 1–5). As it stands, the Beatitude calls for very little comment, because the words employed bear the ordinary meaning which we still give them in daily life, and the statement as given is as clear and obvious in its meaning as the law in question is simple and inflexible in its action.

The point that the Scientific Christian needs to note is that, as usual, the vital bearing of the principle covered in this Beatitude lies in its application to the realm of thought. The thing that really matters is that you be merciful in your thought. Kind actions coupled with unkind thoughts are hypocrisy, dictated by fear, or desire for self-glory, or some such motive. They are counterfeits and they bless neither the giver nor the recipient. On the other hand, the true thought about fellowman blesses him spiritually, mentally, and materially; and blesses you too. Let us be merciful in our mental judgments of our brother, for, in truth, we are all one, and the more deeply he seems to err, the more urgent is the need for us to help him with the right thought, and so make it easier for him to get free. You—because you understand the power of the Spiritual Idea, the Christ Truth—have a responsibility that others have not; see that you do not evade it. When his delinquency comes to your notice, remember that the Christ in him is calling out for help to you who are enlightened—so be merciful.

Because in deed and in truth we are all one, component parts of the living garment of God, you yourself will ultimately receive the same treatment that you mete out to others; you will receive the same merciful help in your own hour of need from those who are farther along the path than you are. Above all is it true that, in freeing others from the weight of your condemnation, you make it possible to absolve yourself from self-condemnation.

BLESSED ARE THE PURE IN HEART: FOR THEY SHALL SEE GOD.

This is one of those wonderful gnomic sayings in which the Bible is so rich. It is nothing less than a summing up in a few words of the whole philosophy of religion. As usual, in the Scriptures, the words are used in a technical sense and cover a far wider meaning than we attach to them in everyday life.

Let us begin by considering what the promise in this Beatitude is. It is nothing less than *to see God*. Now, we know, of course, that God has no corporeal form, and therefore, there is no question of "seeing" Him in the ordinary physical sense in which one might see a human being or an object. If one could see God in this way, He would have to be limited, and therefore, not God. To "see" in the sense referred to here, signifies spiritual perception, and spiritual perception means just that capacity to apprehend the true nature of being which we all so sadly lack.

We live in God's world, but we do not in the least know it as it is. Heaven lies all about us—it is not a distant locality afar off in the skies, but all around us now—but because we are lacking in spiritual perception, we are unable to recognize it; that is to say, we are unable to experience it; and, therefore, so far as we are concerned, we may be said to be shut out of Heaven. We do contact a very tiny fragment of it, and that tiny fragment we call the universe; but even that little bit, we see, for the most part, all awry. Heaven is the religious name for the Presence of God, and Heaven is infinite; but our mental habit leads us to mould our experience into three dimensions only. Heaven is Eternity, but what we know here, we know only serially, in a sequence called "time," which never permits of our comprehending an experience in its entirety. God is Divine Mind, and in that Mind there are no limitations or restrictions at all; yet we see everything distributed in what is called "space," or spaced out—an artificial restriction which continuously inhibits the constant regrouping of our experience that is required by our creative thought.

Heaven is the realm of Spirit, Substance; without age, or discord, or decay; a realm of eternal good; and yet, to our distorted vision, everything is ageing, decaying, wearing out; getting born only to die, blossoming only to fade.

We are very much in the position of a color-blind man in a beautiful flower garden. All around him are glorious colors; but he is quite unaware of them and sees only blacks, whites, and grays. If we suppose him to be also devoid of the sense of smell, we shall see what a very small part of the glory of the garden exists for him. Yet it is all there, if he could but sense it.

This limitation in us is known in theology as the "Fall of Man," and it arises from our using our free will in opposition to the Will of God. "God has made man upright, but he has sought out many inventions." Our task is to surmount these limitations as rapidly as may be, until we reach the point where we can know things as they really are—experience Heaven as it really is. That is what is meant by "seeing God," and seeing him "face-to-face." To see God is to apprehend Truth as it really is, and this is infinite freedom and perfect bliss.

In this wonderful Beatitude we are told exactly how this supreme task is to be accomplished and who they are who shall do it. They are the *pure in heart*. Again, we have to understand that here the words "pure" and "purity" must be taken in a very much wider sense than that which is commonly allotted to them. Purity, in the Bible, means a very great deal more than physical purity—vitally important though that is. In its full and complete sense, purity is recognizing God alone as the only real Cause, and the only real Power in existence. It is what is called elsewhere in the Sermon "the single eye," and it is the Master Key to life. It is nothing less than the secret of escape from all sickness, trouble, and limitation; the overcoming or reversing, in short, of the Fall of Man. And so, our text might well be paraphrased something in this style:

"Blessed are they who recognize God as the only real Cause, and the only real Presence, and the only real Power; not merely in a theoretical or formal way, but practically, and specifically, and wholeheartedly, in all their thoughts, and words, and actions; and not merely in some parts of their lives, but in every nook and corner of their lives and mentalities, keeping nothing back from Him, but bringing their own wills in every last particular into perfect harmony with His Will— for they shall overcome all limitation of time, and space, and matter, and carnal mind; and realize and enjoy the Presence of God forever."

We note how clumsy any paraphrase of a Bible truth always sounds after the matchless grace and conciseness of the inspired text. It is a good thing for each one occasionally to paraphrase in his own language the most familiar texts of Scripture, for this will help him to make clear to his own mind exactly what meaning he is attaching to the text. It will often serve to draw his attention to important meanings which he has hitherto overlooked. Note that Jesus speaks of the *pure in heart*. The word "heart" in the Bible usually means that part of man's mentality which modern psychology knows under the name of the "subconscious mind." This is exceedingly important because it is not sufficient for us to accept the Truth with the conscious mind only. At that stage it is still a mere opinion. It is not until it is accepted by the subconscious mind, and thus assimilated into the whole mentality, that it can make any difference in one's character or life. "As a man thinketh in his heart, so is he." "Keep thy heart with all diligence, for out of it are the issues of life."

Most people, and learned people especially, have all kinds of knowledge that does not in the least affect or improve their practical lives. Doctors know all about hygiene, but often live in an unhealthy way, notwithstanding; and philosophers, who are acquainted with the accumulated wisdom of the ages, and assent to most of it, continue to do foolish and stupid things in their own personal lives, and are unhappy and frustrated in consequence. Now, knowledge such as this is only opinion, or *head* knowledge, as some people call it. It has to become *heart* knowledge, or to be incorporated into the subconscious, before it can really change one.

The modern psychologists in their efforts to "re-educate the subconscious" have the right idea, though they have not yet discovered the true method of doing so, which is by scientific prayer, or the Practice of the Presence of God.

Jesus, of course, thoroughly understood all this, and that is why he stresses the fact that we have to be *pure in heart*.

BLESSED ARE THE PEACEMAKERS: FOR THEY SHALL BE CALLED THE CHILDREN OF GOD.

Here we receive an invaluable practical lesson in the art of prayer—and prayer, be it remembered, is our only means of returning to our communion with God. To the casual reader this Beatitude might sound like a mere conventional religious generalization, even a sententious platitude of the kind too often favored by people who are anxious to be edifying without having anything in particular to say. As a matter of fact, prayer is the only real action in the full sense of the word, because prayer is the only thing that changes one's character. A change in character, or a change in soul, is a real change. When that kind of change takes place, you become a different person and, therefore, for the rest of your life you act in a different way from the way in which you have previously acted, and in which you would have continued to act had you not prayed. In other words, you become a different man. The amount of the difference may be only very slight for each time that you pray: nevertheless it is there, for you cannot pray without making yourself different in some degree. If you should get a very strong realization of the Presence of God with you, it would make a very great and dramatic change in your character, so that, in the twinkling of an eye, your outlook, your habits, your whole life, in fact, would completely change in every respect. Many such cases are on record, both in the East and in the West; the genuine cases of what used to be called "conversion" being instances in point. Because the change caused by prayer is a radical one, Jesus refers to it as being "born again." Since it makes you into a different man, it is actually as though you had been born anew. The word "prayer" should be understood as including any form of communion or attempted communion with God, whether vocal, or purely mental. It includes both affirmative and invocatory prayer, each of which is good in its own place; meditation; and the highest of all forms of prayer, which is contemplation.

In the absence of prayer, all that you can do is to express the character that you have, in whatever circumstances you find yourself. So much is this the case that most of your friends would be prepared to predict beforehand what your conduct would be in various kinds of crises that could arise. Prayer, by changing your character, makes a new reaction possible.

The great essential for success in prayer—for obtaining that sense of the Presence of God, which is the secret of healing oneself and others too; of obtaining inspiration, which is the breath of the soul; of acquiring spiritual development—is that we first attain some degree of true peace of mind. This true, interior soul-peace was known to the mystics as *serenity,* and they are never tired of telling us that serenity is the grand passport to the Presence of God—the sea as smooth as glass that is round about the Great White Throne. This is not to say that one cannot overcome even the most serious difficulties by prayer without having any serenity at all, for of course one can. In fact, the greater the trouble one is in, the less serenity he will able to have, and serenity itself is only to be had by prayer, and by the forgiving of others, and of oneself. But, serenity you must have, before you can make any true spiritual progress; and it is serenity, that fundamental tranquility of soul, that Jesus refers to by the word "peace"—the peace that passes all human understanding.

The *peacemakers* spoken of in this Beatitude are those who make or bring about this true peace, or *serenity,* in their own souls, for it is they who surmount limitation and become actually, and not merely potentially, the *children of God.* This condition of mind is the objective at which Jesus aims in all the instructions which he gives us in the Sermon on the Mount and elsewhere. "Peace I leave with you, my peace I give unto you . . . let not your heart be troubled, neither let it be afraid." As long as there is fear, or resentment, or any trouble in your heart, that is to say, as long as you lack serenity, or *peace,* it is not possible for you to attain very much.

Some degree of serenity is essential to the attainment of any true concentration.

Of course, to be a *peacemaker* in the usual sense of composing the quarrels of other people is an excellent thing; but as all practical people know, an excessively difficult role to fill. By interfering in other people's strife, it is ever so much easier to make things worse than to make them better. Personal opinion is almost certain to enter into your efforts, and personal opinion is exceedingly likely to be wrong. If you can get both of the people concerned to take a new view of the matter in controversy, that, of course, is well; but, otherwise, if you merely bring about a compromise in which they consent to agree from motives of self-interest or as the result of some kind of coercion, then the trouble has only been patched up on the surface, and there is no true peace, because they are not, both of them, satisfied and forgiving.

Once you understand the power of prayer, you will be able really to heal many quarrels in the true way; probably without speaking at all. The silent thought of the All-Power of Love and Wisdom will cause any trouble to melt away almost imperceptibly. Then, whatever arrangement will be best for all parties in the long run will come about under the influence of the Word thus spoken silently.

BLESSED ARE THEY WHICH
ARE PERSECUTED FOR
RIGHTEOUSNESS' SAKE: FOR THEIRS
IS THE KINGDOM OF HEAVEN.

BLESSED ARE YE, WHEN MEN SHALL REVILE
YOU, AND PERSECUTE YOU, AND SHALL
SAY ALL MANNER OF EVIL AGAINST YOU
FALSELY, FOR MY SAKE.

REJOICE, AND BE EXCEEDING GLAD:
FOR GREAT IS YOUR REWARD IN HEAVEN:
FOR SO PERSECUTED
THEY THE PROPHETS WHICH
WERE BEFORE YOU.

In view of what we know about the essential character of the teaching of Jesus, that the Will of God for us is harmony, peace, and joy, and that these things are to be attained by cultivating right thoughts, or "righteousness," this is a very startling statement. Jesus tells us again and again that it is our Father's good pleasure to give us the Kingdom, and that the way in which we are to receive it is by cultivating serenity, or peace of soul. He says that the *peacemakers* who do this, praying in "meekness," shall obtain prosperity, inherit the earth, have their mourning turned into joy, and that, in fact, whatever they shall ask the Father in the manner of this teaching, that will He do. Yet, here we are told that it is blessed to be persecuted as the result of our right thinking, or "righteousness," for that by this means we shall triumph; that it is cause for rejoicing and gladness to be reviled and accused; and that the Prophets and great Illumined Ones suffered these things too.

All this is indeed very startling, and it is perfectly correct; only we have to understand that the source of all this persecution is none other than our own selves. No outside persecutor, but only our own lower selves. When we find righteousness or right thinking very difficult—when we are very strongly tempted to hold the wrong thoughts about some situation, or some person, or about ourselves; to give way to fear, or anger, or despondency—then we are being *persecuted for righteousness' sake,* and this is for us an extremely fortunate or blessed condition, for it is in such moments that we are really advancing. Every spiritual treatment or scientific prayer involves a tussle with our own lower self, which wishes to indulge the old habit of thought, and, in fact, persecutes and reviles us—if we like to put the thing dramatically in the Oriental way. All the great Prophets and Enlightened Ones of the race who ultimately overcame, did so by just such struggles with themselves, when they were being persecuted by their own lower natures, or the Old Adam. Jesus himself, "who was tempted in all respects like as we are," had to meet this "persecution" more than once; especially in the Garden of Gethsemane, and, for a few moments, on the Cross itself. Now, since these combats with the lower self have to be fought out sooner or later, then the sooner they are over and done with the better, and so, relatively speaking, they are great blessings.

Note carefully that there is no virtue or advantage whatever in being persecuted or annoyed by other people. Nothing can come into our experience unless it finds something in us with which it is attuned; and so, to have trouble and difficulty is only a sign that our own mentality needs clearing up; *for what you see at any time is nothing but your own concept.* There is at this point a grave danger for weak, or vain, or self-righteous people. Because others do not treat them just as they would like to be treated, because they do not get consideration that they probably do not deserve, they are often inclined to claim that they are being "persecuted" on account of their spiritual superiority, and to give themselves absurd airs on this ground. This is a pathetic fallacy. In consequence of the great Law of Life, of which the whole Sermon on the Mount is an exposition, we can get only what belongs to us at any time, and nobody can prevent our getting that; and so all persecution and hindrance are absolutely from within.

Despite the sentimental tradition which clings about it, there is no virtue in martyrdom. Did the martyr but possess a sufficient understanding of Truth, it would not be necessary for him to undergo that experience. Jesus was not a "martyr." He could have saved himself at any time had he wished to avoid the crucifixion. It was necessary that someone should triumph over death, having actually died, to make that demonstration possible for us. But he deliberately chose to do a certain work for us in his own way, and was not martyred. We must not in any way depreciate the splendid courage and devotion and heroic self-sacrifice of the martyrs of all ages; but we have to see that their understanding was incomplete, or they would not have been martyred. If you fix your attention on martyrdom, regarding it, as so many did, as the highest good, you will—as with anything upon which you fix your attention—tend to bring it to yourself. While we may well envy them the moral and spiritual heights which they did attain, we know that, had the martyrs "loved" their enemies sufficiently—loved them, that is to say, in the scientific sense of knowing the Truth about them—then the Roman persecutor, even Nero himself, would have opened the doors of their prison; and the fanatic of the Inquisition would have come to reconsider his cause.

CHAPTER THREE

AS A MAN
THINKETH

*Ye are the salt of the earth: but if the salt have lost his savour,
wherewith shall it be salted? It is thenceforth good for nothing, but
to be cast out, and to be trodden under foot of men.*

*Ye are the light of the world. A city that is set on an hill cannot
be hid.*

*Neither do men light a candle, and put it under a bushel, but on a
candlestick; and it giveth light unto all that are in the house.*

*Let your light so shine before men, that they may see your good
works, and glorify your Father which is in heaven.*

—MATTHEW V

I n this wonderful passage Jesus is addressing those who have awakened to the understanding of material bondage, and have acquired some spiritual understanding of the nature of Being. That is to say, he is addressing those who understand the meaning of the Allness of God or Good, and the powerlessness of evil in the face of Truth. Such people he describes as being *the salt of the earth, and the light of the world;* and, indeed, that is not too much to claim for those who understand the Truth, and who *really live the life that corresponds to it.* It is possible, and in fact, only too easy, to accept these vital principles as being true; to love the beauty in them; and yet not to put them consistently into practice in one's own life; but this is a perilous attitude, for in that case *the salt has lost its savour,* and is good for nothing but to be cast out and trodden underfoot.

If you understand and accept the teachings of Jesus; and if you make every effort to practice them in every department of your own daily life; if you seek systematically to destroy in yourself everything which you know should not be there, things such as selfishness, pride, vanity, sensuality, self-righteousness, jealousy, self-pity, resentment, condemnation, and so forth—not feeding or nourishing them by giving in to them, but starving them to death by refusing them expression; if you extend the right thought loyally to every person or thing within your ken, especially to the people or things you dislike; then you are worthy to be called *the salt of the earth.*

If you truly live this life, then it does not in the least matter what your present circumstances may be, or what difficulties you may have to struggle against, you will triumph over them all—you will make your demonstration. And not only will you make your own demonstration, in the quickest possible time, but you will be, and in a very positive and literal sense, a healing and illuminating influence on all around you, and a blessing to the whole human race. You will be a blessing to men and women in remote places and times, men and women of whom you have never heard, and who will never hear of you—a *light of the world,* in fact, startling and wonderful as that may sound.

The state of your soul is always expressed in your outer conditions and in the intangible influence which you radiate at large. There is a Cosmic Law that nothing can permanently deny its own nature. Emerson said: "What you are shouts so loudly that I cannot hear what you say." In the Bible, the "city" always stands for consciousness, and the "hill," or "mountain," always means prayer or spiritual activity. "I will lift up mine eyes unto the hills from whence cometh my help." "Except the Lord keep the city, the watchman waketh but in vain." The soul that is built upon prayer cannot be hidden; it shines out brightly through the life that it lives. It speaks for itself, but in utter silence, and does much of its best work unconsciously. Its mere presence heals and blesses all around it without special effort.

Never try to force other people to accept Spiritual Truth. Instead, see to it that they are so favorably impressed by your own life and conduct, and the peace and joy that radiate from you, that they will come running to you of their own accord, begging you to give them the wonderful thing that you have. "I (the Christ Truth) if I be lifted up, will draw all men unto me." To do this is to make your soul truly the *city upon a hill that cannot be hidden* because it is the Golden City, the City of God. This is to *let your light shine* to the glorifying of your Father which is in Heaven.

> *Think not that I am come to destroy the law, or the prophets: I am not come to destroy, but to fulfil.*
>
> *For verily I say unto you, Till heaven and earth pass, one jot or one tittle shall in no wise pass from the law, till all be fulfilled.*
>
> *Whosoever therefore shall break one of these least commandments, and shall teach men so, he shall be called the least in the kingdom of heaven: but whosoever shall do and teach them, the same shall be called great in the kingdom of heaven.*
>
> *For I say unto you, That except your righteousness shall exceed the righteousness of the scribes and Pharisees, ye shall in no case enter into the kingdom of heaven.*
>
> —MATTHEW V

True Christianity is an entirely positive influence. It comes into a man's life to enlarge and enrich it, to make it fuller and wider and better; never to restrict it. You cannot lose anything that is worth having through acquiring a knowledge of the Truth. Sacrifice there has to be, but it is only sacrifice of the things that one is much happier without—never of anything that is really worth having. Many people have the idea that getting a better knowledge of God will mean giving up things that they will regret losing. One girl said: "I mean to take up religion later on when I am older, but I want to enjoy myself for a while first." This, however, is to miss the whole point. The things one has to sacrifice are selfishness, fear, and belief in necessary limitation of any kind. Above all, one has to sacrifice the belief that there is any power or endurance in evil apart from the power that we ourselves give it by believing in it. Drawing near to God would not have caused this girl to lose any enjoyment, but rather she would have gained immeasurably in happiness. It is quite true that as her consciousness changed she would probably have found that certain forms of pleasure-hunting no longer attracted her. This would probably have happened, but there would have been ample compensation in the new light that would be thrown upon every phase of her life, and in the wonderful new aspects that the world would begin to wear for her. It is only things not worth having that would disappear under the action of Truth.

If, on the other hand, anyone were so insane as to suppose that the knowledge of the Truth of Being could put him "above" the moral law, in the sense of authorizing him to break it, he would speedily discover that he had made a tragic mistake. The more spiritual knowledge that one possesses, the more severe is the punishment which he brings upon himself by any infraction of the moral law. The Christian cannot afford to be less careful than others in observing the whole moral code in every nook and cranny of his life; he has, on the contrary, to be very much more careful than other people. Indeed, all real spiritual understanding must necessarily be accompanied by definite moral improvement. A theoretical acceptance of the letter of Truth might go with moral carelessness (greatly to the peril of the delinquent), but it is utterly impossible to make any real spiritual progress unless you are honestly trying your very best to live the life. It is utterly impossible to divorce true spiritual knowledge from right conduct.

A "jot" (the Greek iota) means "yod," the smallest letter in the Hebrew alphabet. The "tittle" (really "little horn") is one of those tiny spurs or projections that distinguish one Hebrew letter from another. The thought is that not only the letter of the moral law is to be kept, but the minutest detail of the letter. We have to exemplify not merely common morality, but the highest standards of honor.

The Scribes and the Pharisees, in spite of their defects, were for the most part worthy men leading strictly moral lives according to their lights. Unfortunately, they had only the letter of the law, but that letter they usually kept in its entirety, rigorously doing their duty as they saw it. Their faults were the fatal weaknesses of the religious formalist everywhere—spiritual pride and self-righteousness. Of these faults they were sublimely unconscious—that is the deadly malice of these diseases of the soul—and they did strive to fulfil the law as they understood it. Jesus knew this, and he gave them credit for it; and here he warns his followers that unless their practical conduct is in every respect as good as, and even better than, that of these people, they need not suppose that they are making any spiritual headway. Spiritual attainment and the highest standards of conduct must go hand in hand. Unless both are there, neither is there.

As you grow in true spiritual power and understanding you will actually find that many outer rules and regulations will become unnecessary; but this will be because you have really risen above them; never, never, because you have fallen below them. This point in your development, where your understanding of Truth enables you to dispense with certain outer props and regulations, is the Spiritual Coming of Age. When you really are no longer spiritually a minor, you will cease to need some of the outer observances that formerly seemed indispensable; but your resulting life will be purer, truer, freer, and less selfish than it was before; and that is the test.

To give a simple illustration: Some people find that at a certain stage of their progress their mental processes become so orderly and clarified that, with a little treatment, they can go through their day's work, keep all their appointments, and discharge all their duties without bothering to consult the clock or needing to carry a watch. Now it has sometimes happened that one of their friends, knowing about this and desiring to emulate them, has taken the simple step of leaving his watch at home and ignoring the clock, with the result that he is late for all of his appointments, thus upsetting his own day's work and that of other people too, whose convenience he did not trouble to study. When the student is spiritually ready to dispense with his watch, he will find himself doing the right thing at the right time without thinking about a watch at all; whereas, when he has to make special arrangements to discard his watch, and then finds himself late for engagements, it is proof that he is not yet ready to demonstrate in that particular. The proper course for such a person is to carry a watch, work to a timetable, and devote his treatments to things that really matter, such as healing himself and others, overcoming sin, working for understanding and wisdom, and so on. So it is with the larger issues of life. This Spiritual Coming of Age cannot be hurried or forced, but must appear in its own good time, when the consciousness is ready, exactly as the flowering of a bulb can only be the result of natural growth. You have to demonstrate where you are. Let this be for frontlets between your eyes, and write it upon the doorposts of your heart—*you have to demonstrate*

where you are. To seek to demonstrate beyond your understanding is not spiritual. Spiritual development is a matter of
growth, and he that believeth shall not unwisely make haste.
Fix your attention wholeheartedly upon spiritual things, and
meanwhile do all that needs to be done in the ordinary way;
and without consciously trying to make haste you will be
amazed to discover the pace at which your soul has hastened.

To take a simple example: Suppose that in a street ac-
cident you find that a man has severed an artery, and the
blood is spurting out. The normal course of things is that
unless this bleeding is stopped the victim will die within a
few minutes. Now, what is the spiritual attitude to take in
such a case? Well, it is perfectly simple. Immediately you
perceive what has happened; you must *turn the other cheek*
by knowing the Truth of the Omnipresence of God. If you
get this clear enough, as Jesus would, for instance, the severed artery will immediately be healed, and there will be
nothing more to be done. It is exceedingly unlikely, however, that you will get your realization clear enough for this,
and so—demonstrating where you are—you must take the
usual steps to save the man's life by immediately improvis-
ing a tourniquet, or whatever the proper procedure may be.

Or, again, suppose that a child falls into the canal when
you are passing by. Once more, the appropriate action will
be to "speak the Word," and once more, if you have sufficient Spiritual Power, that child will immediately be seen

in safety; but if not, then—demonstrating where you are—you must proceed to rescue him in whatever is the best way; diving in if that should be necessary, and praying as you act.

But, what of the man who is conscious of considerable moral imperfection, perhaps of the habit of grave sin, and is at the same time sincerely desirous of spiritual growth? Is he to relinquish the quest for spiritual knowledge until he has first reformed his conduct? By no means. As a matter of fact, any attempt to improve himself morally without spiritual growth is foredoomed to failure. No more can a man—to use Lincoln's phrase—raise himself off the ground by pulling on his own bootstraps, than the sinner can reform himself by his own personal efforts. The only result of relying upon himself in such cases will be repeated failure, consequent discouragement, and probably ultimate despair of doing any good. The one thing for such a person to do is to pray regularly, especially at the actual time of temptation, and to throw the responsibility for success upon God. He must carry on in this way, no matter how many times he may fail; and, if he continues to pray, and especially if he prays in the scientific way, he will, as a matter of fact, very soon find that the power of evil has been broken, and that he is free from that particular sin. To pray scientifically is to keep affirming that God is helping him, that the temptation has no power against him, and constantly to claim that his own real nature is spiritual and perfect. This is ever so much more powerful than merely to invoke the help of God. In this way moral regeneration and spiritual unfoldment will go hand in hand. The Christian life does not require that we possess perfection of character, or else, which of us would be able to live it? What it does require is honest, genuine striving for that perfection.

> *Ye have heard that it was said by them of old time, Thou shalt not kill; and whosoever shall kill shall be in danger of the judgment:*
>
> *But I say unto you, That whosoever is angry with his brother without a cause shall be in danger of the judgment: and whosoever shall say to his brother, Raca, shall be in danger of the council: but whosoever shall say, Thou fool, shall be in danger of hell fire.*
>
> *Therefore if thou bring thy gift to the altar, and there rememberest that thy brother hath ought against thee:*
>
> *Leave there thy gift before the altar, and go thy way; first be reconciled to thy brother, and then come and offer thy gift.*
>
> —MATTHEW V

The Old Law, dealing as it did with an earlier and lower state of the race consciousness, concerned itself necessarily with external things, for man's apparent evolution is from the outer to the inner, just as his fundamental spiritual growth is from the inner to the outer. He begins by giving his attention exclusively to externals, thinking to find in them cause as well as effect; but as he progresses, the truth gradually dawns upon him that outer things are but the finished article, the result of causes and happenings on the inner; and when he has reached this stage, he has started definitely upon the search for God. So the Old Law concerned itself, at least in the letter, almost altogether with external observances, and it was satisfied if these were fulfilled. It said "Thou shalt not kill," and, provided man did not murder, he kept the law, regardless of how much he may have desired to commit murder or how bitterly he might still hate his enemy. It said "Thou shalt not steal," and provided he did not appropriate his neighbor's property, he was held to have fulfilled the law, irrespective of what he felt about it.

Jesus came to carry the human race forward to the next great step, the most important step of all, which can indeed be the final step in the overcoming of all our limitations, if only we can understand clearly what that step implies, and take it. The heart of the whole Sermon on the Mount, which is itself the essence of the Christian message, is the insistence upon the need for this very step—the understanding that outer conformity, absolutely essential as it is, is no longer sufficient in itself, but that now, if we are to "come of age" spiritually, we have not merely to conform outwardly to outer rules, but to change the inner man too.

The Old Law said "Thou shalt not kill," but Jesus says that even to want to kill, nay, even to be angry with your brother, is sufficient to keep you out of the Kingdom of Heaven; as, of course, it is. It was a distinct gain when primitive, barbarous people could be persuaded not to murder those who had offended them, but to develop sufficient self-control to master their anger. Spiritual demonstration demands that anger itself be overcome. It is simply not possible to get any experience of God worth talking about, or to exercise very much spiritual power in the way of healing, unless and until you have got rid of resentment and condemnation concerning your brother man. Until you are prepared to get rid of this sort of thing, your prayers will have very little effect. It may boldly be said that in prayer, the more love, the more power; and this is why people of developed spiritual perception take such constant pains to keep themselves free from thoughts of criticism and condemnation. They know that they can have either their demonstration or their indignation, but that they cannot have both; and so they do not waste time in trying to.

Indignation, resentment, the desire to punish other people or to see them punished, the desire to "get even," the feeling "it serves him right"—all these things form a quite impenetrable barrier to spiritual power or progress. Jesus, dramatizing the thing in the Oriental way, says that if you are bringing a gift to the altar, and you remember that your brother has anything against you, you must put down your gift without attempting to offer it, and go away and first make peace with your brother, and then, when you have done that, your offering will be acceptable. It was the custom, as we all know, to take gifts of various kinds to the Temple, from bulls and cows down to doves and offerings of incense, or, where it might be more convenient, an offering of money equivalent in value to these things. Now, under the New Law, or Christian dispensation, our altar is our own consciousness, and our offerings are our prayers and treatments. Our "burnt sacrifices" are the error thoughts which we destroy or burn away in spiritual treatment. And so Jesus says that if, when we are about to pray, or remember that we have any wrong thoughts or hard feelings about our brother man, no matter who he may be, and irrespective of whether the object of our hostile thought be an individual or a body of people, we must pause there and treat ourselves until we have got rid of this sense of hostility, and have once more restored the seamless garment of our spiritual integrity.

Jesus builds up this tremendous lesson, again in the Oriental tradition, by employing a series of steps—three in this case. He says first that whoever is angry with his brother shall be in danger; second, that to be really or seriously—one may say vindictively—hostile to another, is to be in grave danger; and finally, that to hold so low an opinion about a fellow creature as to allow ourselves to consider him to be outside the pale, so to speak, is to shut ourselves off from any hope of spiritual fruit while we remain in this state of mind. To call a man a "fool" in this sense means that we consider that no good is to be expected from him; and to do this is to bring very serious consequences upon ourselves.

Note carefully that the Authorized, or King James version of the Bible, which is by far the best all-round edition for spiritual purposes, here makes a serious error, which has been corrected in the Revised version. It makes Jesus say, "Whosoever is angry with his brother *without a cause,*" which is a manifest absurdity. No sane person gets angry without what he deems to be a cause, however trifling or irrelevant the cause that he assigns may be. What Jesus said, of course, was that whoever is angry with his brother under any circumstances is in danger.

> *Agree with thine adversary quickly, while thou art in the way with him; lest at any time the adversary deliver thee to the judge, and the judge deliver thee to the officer, and thou be cast into prison.*
>
> *Verily I say unto thee, Thou shalt by no means come out thence, till thou hast paid the uttermost farthing.*
> —MATTHEW V

This paragraph is of the utmost practical importance; Jesus is stressing here the instruction contained in his injunction to "watch and pray." It is ever so much easier to overcome a difficulty if you tackle it immediately, at its first appearance, than it will be after the trouble has had some little time to establish itself in your mentality—to dig itself in, as the soldiers say. Soldiers know that as long as troops are marching across open ground it is not hard for the enemy to scatter and destroy them; but once let them dig into the ground and entrench themselves, and they become exceedingly difficult to remove. So it is with evil. The moment it presents itself to your attention, you should immediately turn it out, repudiate it, refuse to accept it; and by quietly affirming the Truth, give it no chance to dig itself in. If you do this, you will find that it will have little or no power over you. This procedure will involve a tussle, and it may appear for a little while that the enemy is gaining ground; but, provided you have tackled him in the very beginning, he will presently disappear and you will be left victorious.

On the other hand, by accepting the error and *by thinking about it,* you are incorporating it into your mentality, and, if you go on doing this for long enough, it may be exceedingly difficult to get rid of it. Most of us realize this to our cost. We find it comparatively easy, once we have learned to pray scientifically, to overcome new difficulties as they present themselves; but the older ones whose position we have fortified by long acceptance are difficult to dislodge.

Jesus, in accordance with his usual custom when he

wished to drive home a particularly important point, employed a graphic illustration from the everyday life of the people around him. In those times the law governing debtors was extremely severe. When a man found himself in debt, it strongly behooved him to come to terms with his creditor by any acceptable means, and as quickly as possible. Even at the present day it is highly important for the debtor to keep his case from coming into court if possible—because there are such things as costs. These are added to the original debt, and the longer the case drags on the more do lawyers' fees, court dues, and expenses of various kinds accumulate, all piled on top of the debt proper. Indeed, cases are cited where the costs involved in legal proceedings actually exceeded the original debt itself. So it is with the various difficulties that present themselves to us in our daily lives. The original difficulty as it first appeared usually becomes multiplied many times by our wrong thoughts concerning it, and we do not go free until the whole debt is cleared. By coming to terms with the adversary in the first place, that is to say, by getting our thought right immediately concerning the difficulty, we incur no "costs" and the transaction remains a simple one.

Let us suppose that you find yourself sneezing. If you say "There, now I have caught cold again; now I am in for it!" and then proceed, as people so often do, to dwell upon the thought that you have caught cold, and on the various inconveniences that will probably follow upon that, you are giving the trouble the opportunity to dig itself in to your mentality. People often go on from this to indulge in quite a meditation upon sickness in general, and colds in particular. They will think over the previous few days to discover *when* they caught cold, and they will probably decide with considerable satisfaction that it must be due to that open window on Tuesday, or to sitting, on Wednesday, in the company of a friend who already had a cold; and so forth. Then perhaps they go on to think over several so-called remedies which, however, they have found in the past to be useless. Very frequently they will actually speculate as to how long the coming cold will probably last, usually appointing some definite time such as ten days or two weeks, which, for some reason or other, they suppose to be the natural duration of a cold. In certain cases they even go beyond this, having built up a habit of associating certain secondary ailments with the cold proper, such as bronchitis, temporary deafness, stomach trouble, or whatnot. Now we have seen that this is the very way in which to produce all these things and, therefore, it follows as a natural consequence that, in due order, they put in their appearance as per schedule.

If such a person has some general knowledge of Truth, he will, after thinking in this way for some time, begin to treat himself spiritually as best he can. But by this time he will have amplified the error so strongly, will have allowed it so to dig itself in, that the handling of his cold will be really quite a difficult business. If, upon the error first presenting itself to his consciousness—if, that is to say, at the first moment that the possibility of catching cold occurred to him, either through sneezing or feeling chilly—he had immediately rejected it, claimed his dominion, and affirmed the Truth, that would probably have been the last of the matter, or, at least, the whole thing would have been over in a few hours.

Precisely the same rule applies to any other form of error thought. Business or family difficulties should be handled in exactly the same way. Let us suppose that upon opening your morning mail you find bad news concerning business affairs. It may be that you find a notice informing you that the bank in which most or all of your money is deposited has failed. Again, the usual thing in such cases is to accept the worst and to dwell upon it at almost any length. Many people in such a case would quite saturate themselves with the thought of ruin by thinking over it all day long and probably all night long too, and by discussing it in all its details with other people and rehearsing every kind of trouble and difficulty that might come to them as the result of the occurrence. In addition to all this, there would, in many cases, be bitter resentment and condemnation towards the people—bank officials, and so on—who would be held to be responsible. Now, even a very slight knowledge of the causative power of our thoughts will show us what the result of all this must inevitably be. It must be to increase and multiply the trouble, and make it more and more difficult to escape from it.

Of course, in such a case, a student of the Jesus Christ teaching would sooner or later start to drive all such thoughts out of his mentality, substituting for them his knowledge of the true Law of Being. It may be, however, that having been taken off his guard by the suddenness and seriousness of the blow, it will be some time before he begins to handle the problem in the light of Truth; and it is this delay that will increase his difficulty many times. The proper thing to do, according to Jesus, is, immediately he becomes aware of the bad news, to turn to God—his real support—to refuse to accept the suggestion of trouble as binding upon him; and literally to drive the thought of loss and danger right out of his consciousness, together with the fear and the resentment that go with it. If he does this, working steadily until his peace of mind is restored, he will presently find himself safely out of his difficulty. In some way or other the trouble will disappear, and his fortunes will be restored. Either the bank will speedily recover itself—and there is no reason at all why one person's prayer should not save the bank and the fortunes of thousands—or, if this for any reason be not possible, he will find that a sum of money equal to or greater than the one he lost in the bank will come to him from some other and probably quite unexpected direction. "Whosoever shall call upon the name of the Lord shall be saved."

The same principle would, of course, apply equally to any kind of difficulty whatever, since universal harmony is the true Law of Being. A dispute, or quarrel, or misunderstanding should be handled in the same way from the first moment you become aware of it.

> *Ye have heard that it was said by them of old time, Thou shalt not commit adultery:*
>
> *But I say unto you, That whosoever looketh on a woman to lust after her hath committed adultery with her already in his heart.*
>
> —MATTHEW V

In this unforgettable paragraph, Jesus stresses the Master Truth, so utterly fundamental, yet so unsuspected by the world at large, that what really matters is thought. People have always been accustomed to suppose that as long as their deeds conformed to the law, they have done all that can be reasonably expected of them, and that their thoughts and feelings are of little importance, and that in any case these are their own business exclusively. But we know now that any outward act is but the sequel to a thought, and that the type of thought which we allow to become habitual will sooner or later find expression on the plane of action. We understand now, in the light of Scientific Christianity, that thoughts literally are things, and that our choice of conduct really lies in our choice of the kind of thought that we permit to occupy the stage of our mind. In other words, we have discovered that a wrong thought is just as destructive an act as a wrong deed.

The logical consequence of this undeniable fact is very startling. It means that if you entertain covetous thoughts for your neighbor's money, you are a thief at heart, even though you may not yet have put your hand in the till; and if you continue to entertain such thoughts, it is only a question of time before you will rob him. If you willingly nourish hatred, you are a murderer at heart, even though your hands have not moved to kill. The adulterer at heart is corrupting his soul even though his impure thought is never expressed on the physical plane. Lust, jealousy, vengeance, mentally entertained, carry the soul's consent; and this soul-consent is the malice of sin, whether the corresponding outer acts be yet materialized or not. "Keep thy heart with all diligence, for out of it are the issues of life."

CHAPTER FOUR

RESIST
NOT EVIL

And if thy right eye offend thee, pluck it out, and cast it from thee:
for it is profitable for thee that one of thy members should perish,
and not that thy whole body should be cast into hell.

 And if thy right hand offend thee, cut it off, and cast it from thee: for
it is profitable for thee that one of thy members should perish,
and not that thy whole body should be cast into hell.

—MATTHEW V

The soul's integrity is the one and only thing that matters. We have no problem but to bring this about, no need but to obtain this; for having this, we have all. And so Jesus in his teaching is almost exclusively concerned in impressing us with the overwhelming fact of its importance, and with instructing us in how we are to accomplish it. He insists that positively no sacrifice can be too great to insure the integrity of one's soul. Anything, *anything* that stands in the way of that, must be given up. Cost what it will, involve what it may, the integrity of the soul must be preserved; for all other things—conduct, health, prosperity, life itself—follow upon that. Better sacrifice your right eye itself, he says, or cut off your very right hand, if need be, that your soul may obtain the clarity of understanding that is salvation.

It matters not what the thing may be that is standing between us and our true contact with God—*it must go.* It may be a sin, it may be an old grudge left unforgiven, it may be stark greed for the things of this world; but whatever it is, it must go. Such things as these, however, are so obvious that at least the transgressor is certain to be aware of them; it is the subtle things like self-love and his brother self-righteousness, spiritual pride, and so forth, that are most difficult for the self to detect and to exercise—but it must be done. It sometimes happens that the practice of a certain profession,

or the association with certain people, or membership of some particular body is what is standing in our way; and if such is the case, we must not hesitate; the price must be paid.

It hath been said, Whosoever shall put away his wife, let him give her a writing of divorcement:

But I say unto you, That whosoever shall put away his wife, saving for the cause of fornication, causeth her to commit adultery: and whosoever shall marry her that is divorced committeth adultery.

—MATTHEW V

We are told that in those days divorces were granted by the Rabbinical law on the most trifling grounds. Married people who were not getting on together as well as they would have liked, were too prone to run away from that problem by obtaining an easy dissolution, and then trying their luck with someone else. Now we understand that no permanent happiness can be obtained in this way. As long as you are running away from your problem, you will continue to meet it in a new guise at every turn in the road. The scientific solution is to meet your difficulty where you are by means of spiritual treatment or scientific prayer. This

applies to problems concerning marriage quite as much as, if not more than, to problems of any other kind. As none of us is perfect, and the complainant is certain to have his or her own faults no less than the delinquent, he or she should endeavor, if it can possibly be done, to make the present marriage a success by persistently knowing the Spiritual Truth about both parties. If the aggrieved partner will steadfastly see the Christ Truth about the other one, then, in nearly every case a happy solution will be the outcome. I have known a number of instances where marriages which were on the point of being dissolved were saved in this way with the most satisfactory results. One woman said, after a few months of handling her problem spiritually, "The man I was going to divorce has disappeared; and the man whom I married has come back. We are perfectly happy again."

Just as in running from one business position to another, or from one home to another, without first having brought about a change in consciousness, we find ourselves but re-peating the old conditions in a slightly different form, so, as a rule, people who divorce freely, trying marriage after marriage, are apt to finish up as dissatisfied as they began. The general rule in Truth is, fight out your problem where you are, with prayer.

Nevertheless, there is a limit to what a man or woman can be expected to put up with in marriage, and in excep-

tional cases, no doubt, the lesser evil is a dissolution; but this should be only the last resort. Jesus, we know, consistently refrained from laying down hard-and-fast rules and regulations for the details of our conduct, knowing that if our principles were right, such things would take care of themselves without fail; and we may be sure that, with his supremely practical and common-sense handling of human problems, he would have given the wise and merciful decision in any particular case. The woman taken in adultery, for instance, who should absolutely have been stoned to death under the law of Moses, still current at that time, was forgiven and dismissed in peace by him, in the teeth of the written Scripture. At any rate those who are in any doubt concerning their own conduct in this matter have a simple remedy—they should treat for guidance in their conduct. They should claim that Divine Wisdom is illumining their understanding and directing their actions in the matter, and avoid taking any definite steps until they find a clear leading in their own consciousness.

The general rule is still good for all conditions in life: Do not try to divorce or amputate the inharmony, but let it dissolve away of itself under treatment. That is what was done by the woman who said that the man she married had come back; and she considers her demonstration a perfect one.

Again, ye have heard that it hath been said by them of old time,
Thou shalt not forswear thyself, but shalt perform unto the Lord
thine oaths:

But I say unto you, Swear not at all; neither by heaven; for it
is God's throne;

Nor by the earth; for it is his footstool; neither by Jerusalem;
for it is the city of the great King.

Neither shalt thou swear by thy head, because thou canst not
make one hair white or black.

But let your communication be, Yea, yea; Nay, nay: for
whatsoever is more than these cometh of evil.

—MATTHEW V

Swear not at all is one of the cardinal points in the teaching
of Jesus. It means, briefly, that you are not to take vows.
You are not to mortgage your future conduct in advance; to
undertake to do or to refrain from doing something tomorrow, or next year, or thirty years hence. You are not in any
way to seek to fix your conduct or your belief for tomorrow
while it is yet today—for "sufficient unto the day is the evil
thereof." It is an absolutely vital part of his teaching that you
are constantly to seek direct inspirational contact with God,
constantly to keep yourself an open channel for the pouring
out of the Holy Spirit into manifestation through you. Now,
if you make up your mind in advance as to what you shall do

or shall not do, shall believe or shall not believe, shall think or shall not think, shall be or shall not be, tomorrow, or next year, or for the rest of your life—and especially when you crystallize this determination by a solemn act of the will like a vow—you are not leaving yourself open to the action of the Paraclete; but you are, by that very act, shutting Him out. If you are to receive the guidance of God, Divine Wisdom, it is absolutely essential that you have an open mind, because it so often happens that the part of wisdom is not in accord with your own personal feelings or present opinions. But if you have taken a vow or made a promise concerning your soul, for tomorrow, you are no longer uncommitted; and unless you are uncommitted, the action of the Holy Spirit cannot take place. This, in fact, is nothing less than the sin against the Holy Ghost of which the Bible speaks, which has caused so much terror to sensitive hearts, and concerning which there seems to be a very general misunderstanding.

What is the sin against the Holy Ghost? The sin against the Holy Ghost is any action on your part which prevents the activity of the Holy Ghost from taking place in your soul; anything which shuts you off from the ever-fresh energizing action of God that is spiritual life itself. The penalty for this mistake is spiritual stagnation and, since the only remedy in such a case consists in the direct action of the Holy Spirit, and this mistake in itself tends to prevent that very action from taking place, a condition of vicious deadlock results. Now it is obvious that this condition must necessarily remain as long as the mistake is persisted in, and so, in this sense, the sin is unforgivable. The problem cannot be solved in any way until the victim is prepared to change his attitude. The symptoms of this malady are spiritual stagnation, and all-round failure to demonstrate, and these are only too often accompanied by much self-righteousness and spiritual pride.

Of course, Jesus does not mean that you are not to enter into ordinary business engagements, such as taking up the lease of a house, signing an agreement for certain services, entering into partnership, and so on. Nor does he mean that the ordinary oath administered in a court of law is inadmissible. These things are matters of legal convenience for the transaction of business between man and man, and they are right and necessary in an ordered society. The Sermon on the Mount, as we have seen, is a treatise on the *spiritual* life, for the spiritual life controls all the rest. One who understands the spiritual teaching of Jesus, and practices it, will be in no danger of breaking honorable agreements. He will be an ideal tenant, a desirable business partner, and a reliable witness in court.

Many of the churches still require their ministers, upon ordination—and usually while they are still quite young, immature minds—solemnly to promise or vow that they will, for the whole of their future lives, continue to believe the doctrines of their particular sect; and this is what Jesus especially wished to prevent. If one is praying every day, as he should, for enlightenment and guidance, the one certain thing is that he will *not* go on holding to the same ideas as he grows older, but that he will be continually revising, enlarging, and expanding them. He will die daily, as the man he is, to be reborn bigger and wiser and better on the morrow.

Other religious movements require even their private members to accept some kind of Rule Book or written instructions for their perpetual guidance; but any such thing is quite fatal, because it automatically shuts out the action of the Holy Spirit. In this respect some of the youngest and most up-to-date churches are just as sadly unspiritual as the oldest ones. You must always be perfectly free at any moment to conduct the affairs of your soul as the action of Divine Wisdom may lead you; to pray or not to pray, to pray in this way or that way, and for this or that purpose; to read or not to read any book; to attend or not to attend any church or meeting, as you may feel led.

In the same deadly spirit some teachers forbid their students to read any religious books except those of their own school. This is such an appalling crime against the very life of the soul that no words can be found adequately to characterize it.

On the whole, the most important application of this injunction against making hard-and-fast rules lies in the matter of our prayers. Many people have made rigid rules for the conduct of their personal prayers or devotions; but these are sure to destroy the spirit of the thing sooner or later. People say: "I always start with the Lord's Prayer," or a certain Psalm, or something else. Others say: "I begin every treatment in such and such a way." All this is a mistake. You should always pray as you feel led to do by the action of the Holy Spirit in your soul at the moment. It is the spontaneous prayer, the thought that is "given" to you at the moment, that carries power. A thought that is "given" to you in this way has ten times more power to demonstrate than one that you consciously select for yourself. Remember, however, that it is only hard-and-fast rules that are to be avoided. It is a good thing to have some kind of schedule of prayer to fall back upon at times when nothing better presents itself, and, in fact, most beginners will need a schedule for some time. The essential point is that you must always be ready to drop it at a moment's notice, under the leading of Spirit. People sometimes find themselves in a condition where their prayers appear to be bringing no result, and this is most often due to the fact that they have simply gone stale on fixed forms. If this happens, feel out mentally for inspiration, and then use the first thought that comes; or try dipping into the Bible at random.

This section further teaches us that we must not undertake to bring about particular events or conditions, or particular solutions to our problems—what is technically called "outlining." When you find yourself in difficulties, you should pray for harmony and freedom, and expect to get it; but you should not seek to select the exact arrangement that will come about, or the course that things will take. If you make up your mind very firmly that you are going to get a particular thing, you may, if you have a certain type of mentality, bring it about; but this exercise of will power is almost certain to land you in difficulties—you will get your own way, and then you will bitterly regret it.

Yea, yea, and *nay, nay,* stand for what are called in scientific prayer the Affirmation and the Denial, respectively. These are the Affirmation of Truth and Harmony and the Omnipresence of God in Reality; and the denial of any power in error and limitation.

> *Ye have heard that it hath been said, An eye for an eye, and a tooth for a tooth:*
>
> *But I say unto you, That ye resist not evil: but whosoever shall smite thee on thy right cheek, turn to him the other also.*
>
> *And if any man will sue thee at the law, and take away thy coat, let him have thy cloke also.*
>
> *And whosoever shall compel thee to go a mile, go with him twain.*
>
> *Give to him that asketh thee, and from him that would borrow of thee turn not thou away.*
>
> —MATTHEW V

Jesus is the most revolutionary of all teachers. He turns the world upside down for those who accept his teaching. When once you have accepted the Jesus Christ Message, nothing is ever the same again. All values change radically. The things that one spent time and energy in striving for are felt to be no longer worth the having, while other things that one passed by on the way with scarcely a glance, are discovered to be the only things that really matter. Compared with Jesus, all the so-called revolutionists, radicals, and reformers of history are now seen to have been merely scratching the surface—rearranging unimportant externals—whereas Jesus went down to the root of things and attacked that.

The Old Law, designed to maintain some degree of order, however rough and ready, among a barbarous people—for any kind of law is better than anarchy—had said *an eye for an eye, and a tooth for a tooth*. Whatever man did to man, he should himself be made to suffer by way of punishment. If he killed another, the law would kill him. If he put out another man's eye, his own was put out by the officers of justice. To whatever extent he maimed or wounded another, he himself would be made to suffer too; and this code was better than none, and perhaps not bad as a beginning. For barbarous people, unable to appreciate the abstract idea of justice, unable to look forward beyond the passion of the moment, without imagination to realize an unobvious penalty, this did, no doubt, in most cases furnish an effective check upon primitive instinct. Then, as time went on, and barbarism gradually passed into a settled civilization, this primitive code was slowly modified by public opinion into something at least less obviously brutal.

This was the case as far as public justice was concerned. In private life, however, the ancient code continued to hold sway in men's hearts and minds, even though they no longer perpetrated actual deeds of violence; and it is not exaggerating to say that it has continued to hold sway down to the present hour. The desire to "get even," to get one's own back, to level things up somehow or other, when we have been hurt or have suffered injustice, or witnessed things of which we did not approve, is still with us all—and will remain with us until the time when we definitely take ourselves in hand and destroy it. "Revenge," said Bacon, "is a kind of wild justice," and the natural man with the natural thirst for justice (for true justice is a part of the Divine Harmony, and all men at every stage seem always to have some intuitive conception of the Divine Spiritual Harmony that lies behind appearances) feels that the proper way to restore a balance is the obvious one of paying back the delinquent in his own coin.

But this is precisely the deadly fallacy that lies at the root of all the strife, public and private, in the world. It is the direct cause of international wars, of family feuds and personal quarrels, and, as we shall learn in the study of Scientific Christianity, it is the cause of much, if not most, of our ill health and our other difficulties. Now Jesus reverses this and says that when someone injures you, instead of seeking to get your own back or to repay him in his own coin, you are to do the very opposite—you are to forgive him, and set him free. No matter what the provocation may be, and no matter how many times it is repeated, you are to do this. You are to loose him and let him go, for thus only can you be freed yourself—thus only can you possess your own soul. To return evil for evil, to answer violence with violence and hate with hate, is to start a vicious circle to which there is no ending but the wearing out of your own life and your brother's too.

"Hatred ceases not with hatred," said the Light of Asia, enunciating this great Cosmic Truth many centuries before, and the Light of the World put it in the forefront of his teaching because it is the cornerstone of man's salvation.

This doctrine of "resist not evil" is the great metaphysical secret. To the world—those who do not understand—it sounds like moral suicide, the feeblest surrender to aggression; but in the light of the Jesus Christ revelation it is seen to be superb spiritual strategy. Antagonize any situation, and you give it power against yourself; offer mental nonresistance, and it crumbles away in front of you.

Jesus, as we have seen, is the Master Metaphysician, concerning himself only with states of consciousness, with the thoughts and beliefs that men accept for these are the things that matter, the things that are *causative.* He gives no instructions for details of external conduct, and so the references here to suing at law, to coat and cloak, to lending and borrowing, to turning the other cheek, are illustrative and symbolical of *mental states,* and are not to be taken in the narrow literal sense. This statement is not in any way an endeavor to evade or gloss over a difficult text. We cannot too often remind ourselves that if the thought is right, the deed cannot be wrong; and that a mere deed undertaken from an exterior motive is just as likely to be wrong as right in any particular instance, for there are simply no complete general rules for right conduct. No teacher could ever say that a given act must necessarily be right at any time, because the play of circumstances in human life is too hopelessly complicated for any such prediction. Anyone with the slightest experience of the world knows, for example, that to lend money indiscriminately to anyone who may ask for it is certainly not the part of wisdom, certainly not the part of elementary justice either to oneself or to those who may be dependent upon one, and that it would, in most cases, inflict actual injury instead of benefit upon the would-be borrower. As for turning the other cheek, literally, for a blow, such a proceeding would be in the last degree unlikely to do anything but harm to both parties; and we should note particularly that Jesus, when he was struck in the room of Pilate, did not do this himself; on the contrary, he met his enemies with grave dignity. This instruction about turning the other cheek refers to the changing of one's thought when faced by error, changing from the error to the Truth—and, as a rule, it acts like magic.

If, when someone is behaving badly, instead of thinking of the trouble, you will immediately switch your attention off from the human to the Divine, and concentrate upon God, or upon the Real Spiritual Self of the person in question, you will find—if you really do this—that his conduct will immediately change. This is the secret of handling difficult people, and Jesus understood it thoroughly. If people are troublesome, you have only to change your thought about them, and then they will change too, because your own concept is what you see. This is the true revenge. It has been tried thousands and thousands, perhaps millions of times; and it never fails when properly carried out. It is often quite amusing to see it acting like clockwork. If somebody comes into the room at home, or into the office or shop, or anywhere else, looking as if he meant to make trouble, just try switching your attention straight off to the Divine, instead of sparring up aggressively to meet the difficulty or shrinking away to avoid it, according to your temperament. You will be amused and gratified to see the anger fade away from the subject's face (which will mean that it has faded from his heart too) and quite a different expression take its place. You may find it helpful in the beginning to glance away from him while giving yourself this "treatment," but with a little practice you will be able, so to speak, to look through him to the Truth of Being.

A lady was annoyed by overhearing two men engaged on some repairs outside her window, who, unaware of her proximity, were indulging in very bad language. For a moment a tide of anger and contempt surged up in her mind concerning them, but, remembering this text, she instantly concentrated her attention upon the Divine Presence which she knew to be within each of them—as it is within all men. She saluted the Indwelling Christ in them, to use our modern expression; and instantaneously the offensive language ceased. She said it was as though it had been chopped off with a knife. She must have got a good realization, and in that case it is certain that both men received a substantial spiritual uplift, and may even have been permanently healed of the use of unclean language.

All those of us who have been working in Truth for any length of time could cite many similar cases of harmony suddenly restored by this simple method of Jesus—that of "turning the other cheek." I have myself seen several cases where men, and on two occasions children, were actually fighting, and upon a spectator "turning the cheek" in this manner, this strife ceased like magic. Animals respond even more easily to this treatment than do human beings. I have seen two instances where dogs were fighting savagely and all efforts to separate them had failed, when the realization of the Presence of God's love in all His creatures restored peace. In one case it took several minutes' work; in the other it was practically instantaneous.

It will sometimes happen that you will find yourself in company where the conversation is very negative, sickness and trouble being described and dwelt upon at great length, or perhaps uncharitable statements made concerning absent people. For various reasons it may be difficult for you to withdraw, and if so your duty is clear—you must mentally "turn the other cheek" and thus help both the speakers and their victims.

Let him have thy cloak also, and *go with him twain* are dramatic expressions that still further emphasize the principle of nonresistance in thought to seemingly evil conditions. Meet the attitude of fellow man sympathetically as far as you possibly can, concede every point that is not absolutely essential, and redeem the remainder with the True Thought or Christ. Never surrender to error, of course. But it is the sin and not the sinner that is to be condemned.

Ye have heard that it hath been said, Thou shalt love thy neighbor, and hate thine enemy.

But I say unto you, Love your enemies, bless them that curse you, do good to them that hate you, and pray for them which despitefully use you, and persecute you;

> *That ye may be the children of your Father which is in heaven;*
> *for he maketh his sun to rise on the evil and on the good, and*
> *sendeth rain on the just and on the unjust.*
>
> *For if ye love them which love you, what reward have ye?*
> *do not even the publicans the same?*
>
> *And if ye salute your brethren only, what do ye more than*
> *others? do not even the publicans so?*
>
> —MATTHEW V

Love your enemies, bless them that curse you, do good to them that hate you, and pray for them that despitefully use you, and persecute you. "Hatred ceases not with hatred," is here again the theme; now Jesus puts this fundamental truth in such a plain and simple way that not even the youngest child can misunderstand him. Instead of hating him who seems to be your enemy, as the lower instinct impels man to do, you are to love him. For curses you are to return blessings, and hatred you are to reward with good. For those who actually go to the length of persecuting you, you are to pray, definitely and specifically. Jesus says it as plainly and directly as that; and then, in order to meet everybody on the very simplest level of comprehension, he adds: "If you return love for love, what is there out of the ordinary in that?" Nothing, of course, for anyone would do as much. If you wish to make any real advance you must do much more. You must get rid of all sense of resentment and hostility. You must change your own state of mind until you are conscious only of harmony and peace within yourself, and have a sense of positive goodwill towards all.

This is not merely the best practical policy, but, for the reasons upon which the whole Sermon on the Mount is founded, it is the only policy wherewith you can make any progress at all. Physical health itself, for instance, is not in the long run possible without forgiveness and good-will to everyone, and even your material prosperity will disappear at last unless your soul is free from enmity and condemnation. Indeed, such freedom is the primary requisite for any spiritual progress at all, and anyone with any spiritual sense easily recognizes this when once it has been pointed out to him. Those who have some understanding of what is called the Spiritual Idea find here a wonderful lesson in practical spiritual treatment, or scientific prayer. Quite simply, the Spiritual Ideal is the understanding of the basic fact that good is permanent, omnipresent, and all-powerful; and evil, a temporary, insubstantial belief, without character of its own, which is destroyed by scientific prayer. Thus, what may be called *the secret of spiritual treatment* is not to wrestle with the error, which only gives it further life and power, but to destroy it by withdrawing from it just that very energy of belief that gives it its body. *The only existence it has, is that which you give it by temporarily ensouling it with your thought*. Withdraw this—and it fades into nothingness. You have thought the error into existence, consciously or, more often, unconsciously. Now unthink it. It is always your thinking that matters. Indeed, as Shakespeare says, "There is nothing either good or bad but thinking makes it so." Now, fear, hatred, and resentment are ideas heavily charged with emotion, and these, when added to any difficulty, recharge it with fresh and vigorous life and make it all the more difficult to overcome. Again, the mere rehearsing in thought of any difficulty endows it with new life. Going over old grievances mentally; thinking how badly someone acted at some time, for instance, and recalling the details, has the effect of revivifying that which was quietly expiring of neglect.

With a new difficulty of any kind, it is the reception that you give it mentally, and the attitude that you adopt towards it in your own thought, that completely determine its effect upon you. That is what matters. What matters to you, truly, is not people or things or conditions in themselves, but the thoughts and beliefs that you hold concerning them. It is not the conduct of others, but your own thoughts that make or mar you. You write your own history for tomorrow and for next year by the thoughts that you entertain today. You mold your own life destiny day by day, entirely by the manner in which you react mentally to experience as it comes. Right reaction is the supreme art of life, and Jesus compressed the secret of that art into a sentence when he said: *Resist not evil.*

Resist not evil, spiritually understood, is the grand secret of success in life. A correct understanding of this commandment will lead you out of the Land of Egypt, and out of the House of Bondage; regenerate your body; liberate your soul; and, in short, remake your life from top to bottom. As soon as you resist mentally any undesirable or unwanted circumstance, you thereby endow it with more power—power which it will use against you, and you will have depleted your own resources to that exact extent. Whether you have to meet a physical, or a personal, or a business difficulty, you must not, as people usually do, hurl yourself against it mentally, or even stand stubbornly in the middle of the road saying, "You shall not pass"; but, observe the master rule of Jesus, and *resist not evil.* Refrain from resisting the trouble mentally; that is to say, refuse to feed your own soul-substance into it. Feel out, mentally, for the Presence of God, as you would feel out physically if thrust suddenly into a dark room. Hold your thought steadily to that Presence as being with you, and as being also in the person or the place where the evil has presented itself; that is to say, *turn the other cheek.* If you will do this, the difficulty, whatever it is, the undesirable situation or the trouble that someone is making, will fade away into its native nothingness, and leave you free. This is the true spiritual method of *loving your enemy.*

Love is God and is therefore absolutely all powerful. This is the scientific application of Love, against which nothing evil can stand. It destroys the evil condition and, if a person is concerned, it sets him as well as you free. But to return hate for hate, curse for curse, or fear for aggression, has the effect of amplifying the trouble, much as a feeble sound is multiplied in volume by an amplifier. Meeting hatred with Love in the scientific way is the Royal Christ Road to freedom. This is the perfect method of self-defense in all circumstances. It renders you absolutely invulnerable to any kind of attack.

If someone makes himself personally obnoxious to you, do not resist him in thought. *Resist not evil;* realize the Indwelling Christ in your "enemy," and all will be well. He will cease to trouble you, and either change his attitude or else fade out of your life altogether, besides being spiritually benefited by your action. If you receive bad news, do not resist it in thought. Realize the unchanging nature and infinite harmony of Good ever available, at every point of existence; and things will come right. If you are unhappy in your work, or in your home, do not resist these conditions mentally, or indulge in grumbling, or self-pity, or in recriminations of any kind. Such action will only strengthen that particular embodiment of error; so, *resist not evil.* Feel out mentally for the Presence of Divine Spirit, all around you; affirm its actuality; and claim that you have dominion over all conditions when you speak the Word in the name of I Am That I Am, and you will soon be free.

Loving your enemies in this scientific way is also the key to bodily health, without which it is impossible to possess it. The secret of physical well-being lies in the realization of Divine Life and Divine Love. All physical improvement follows upon this; it does not precede it. Today much is made of the influence of the glands on our bodily health, but our glands themselves are, all of them, governed entirely by our emotions, and thus the way to adjust and regulate the glands is by the cultivation of right feeling. Of course, this must be made to include subconscious feelings, and that can only be done by treatment.

Be ye therefore perfect, even as your Father which is in heaven is perfect.

—MATTHEW V

This command of Jesus is one of the most tremendous things in the whole Bible. Consider carefully what it is that he is saying. He is commanding us to be perfect, even as God Himself is perfect; and, as we know that Jesus will not command the impossible, he has here given his authority to the doctrine that it is possible for man to become Divinely perfect. And, more than this, he is putting it forward as a thing that will have to be actually done. We see, therefore, from this that man cannot possibly be the miserable, hopeless, disinherited child of perdition that theology has too often represented him to be; but that he is even the very offspring of God—our Father which is in Heaven—and potentially Divine and perfect. As Jesus elsewhere puts it, quoting the ancient scripture: "I said, ye are gods; and all of you sons of the Most High." He then added by way of emphasis: "And the scripture cannot be broken."

Now, if we really are the children of God, capable of eternal and flawless perfection, there can be no real power in evil, not even in sin, to keep us permanently in bondage. That is to say, with the right method of working, it can be only a matter of time before we assume our true condition of spiritual salvation; so now let us lose no further time before commencing our upward march. Let us now—at this very moment, if we have not already done so—rise up, like the prodigal son amid the husks of materiality and limitation, and cry, with all confidence in the teachings and promises of Jesus: "I will arise and go unto my Father."

Those who may be discouraged by a sense of their own unworthiness, or lack of understanding, and feel themselves to be indeed "a great way off," should recollect that all the Great Spiritual Teachers have agreed that there is such a thing as "taking the Kingdom of Heaven by storm."

CHAPTER FIVE

TREASURE IN HEAVEN

Take heed that ye do not your alms before men, to be seen of them: otherwise ye have no reward of your Father which is in heaven.

Therefore when thou doest thine alms, do not sound a trumpet before thee, as the hypocrites do in the synagogues and in the streets, that they may have glory of men. Verily I say unto you, They have their reward.

But when thou doest alms, let not thy left hand know what thy right hand doeth:

That thine alms may be in secret: and thy Father which seeth in secret himself shall reward thee openly.

And when thou prayest, thou shalt not be as the hypocrites are: for they love to pray standing in the synagogues and in the corners of the streets, that they may be seen of men. Verily I say unto you, They have their reward.

But thou, when thou prayest, enter into thy closet, and when thou hast shut thy door, pray to thy Father which is in secret; and thy Father which seeth in secret shall reward thee openly.

But when ye pray, use not vain repetitions, as the heathen do: for they think that they shall be heard for their much speaking.

Be not ye therefore like unto them: for your Father knoweth what things ye have need of, before ye ask him.

—MATTHEW VI

The heart of this section of the Sermon is contained in verses 6 and 7, particularly the clause: *Pray to thy Father which is in secret; and thy Father which seeth in secret shall reward thee openly.* The doctrine of the "Secret Place" and its importance as the controlling center of the "Kingdom," is the essential factor of the Jesus Christ teaching.

Man is the ruler of a kingdom, although in most cases he knows it not. That kingdom is nothing less than the world of his own life and experience. The Bible is full of stories of kings and their kingdoms; of wise kings and foolish kings; of wicked kings and righteous kings; of victorious kings and defeated kings; of the rise and fall of kingdoms from every sort of cause. Jesus, in his parabolic teaching, will often take the same idea and use it as a simile. "There was a great king . . . ," he often begins. Now each of these kings is really Everyman, studied in the various aspects of his mental outlook. The Bible is the book of Everyman. It is primarily a textbook of metaphysics, a manual of the soul's development, and everything in the Bible, from Genesis to Revelation, is really concerned with that development; that is to say, the spiritual awakening of the individual. You and your problems are analyzed from every possible angle, and the fundamental lessons of Spiritual Truth are put forward in all sorts of different ways to meet every condition, and every need, and almost every mood of human nature. Sometimes you are a king; sometimes you are fisherman; sometimes a gardener, a weaver, a potter, a merchant, a High Priest, a Captain of Hosts, or a beggar.

It is as a king, the absolute ruler of his own kingdom, that the Sermon on the Mount considers you; for this, after all, is the most complete of all the similes. When you know the Truth of Being, you are, as a literal fact and not merely in a rhetorical sense, the absolute monarch of your own life. You make your own conditions, and you can unmake them. You make and unmake your own health. You attract to yourself certain kinds of people and certain conditions—and others you repel. You attract to yourself riches or poverty, and peace of mind or fear—entirely in accordance with the way in which you govern your kingdom. Of course, the world does not know this. It supposes that the conditions of one's life are largely made for him by outer circumstances, and by other people. It believes that one is at all times liable to unforeseen and unexpected accidents of one sort or another, any one of which may seriously inconvenience or even completely ruin his scheme of life. But the Truth of Being is just the contrary of all this, and, since mankind has nearly always believed the false version, we cannot wonder that history has been so full of mistakes and suffering and trouble.

Nothing but misfortune and confusion could possibly follow from the endeavor to conduct any business on false principles, or to carry out a train of reasoning from a series of erroneous premises—and this is naturally what has happened. Man has suffered because he has been deceived about the nature of life and of himself; and that is why Jesus—the Saviour of the World—said: "Know the Truth, and the Truth shall make you free." That was why he spent the years of his public life in teaching and explaining the Truth; telling us about God and man, and instructing us how to live.

If it is true, as it is, that our difficulties arise from our own wrong thinking, in the present and in the past, it may well be asked, considering the sublime level of consciousness to which Jesus had attained: Why did he have to meet difficulties from time to time—notably his terrible conflict with fear at Gethsemane, and his death upon the cross?

The answer is that the case of Jesus was quite different from that of anyone else, because he suffered, not for his own wrong thinking, but for ours. Owing to his high degree of understanding, he could easily have gone away and transcended quietly, without any suffering, as Moses and Elijah, for instance, had done before him. But he deliberately chose to undertake his awful task in order to help mankind; and he is therefore justly entitled the Saviour of the World.

Now we come to consider this kingdom a little more in detail, and we find that the King's Palace, the office of government, so to say, is nothing less than your own consciousness—your own mentality. This is your very own private cabinet, and the business transacted there is the swirl of thoughts that continually pass across your mind. The "Secret Place of the Most High," the Psalmist calls it, and it is secret because no one but yourself knows what goes on therein. There is privacy, and there is dominion. You have the power to think what thoughts you like. You can choose which thoughts you will accept and which you will reject. You are master there. Whatever thoughts you do elect to dwell upon will presently be expressed in the outer physical world as things and events—but that is your lookout. Having thought certain thoughts, you have no power to change the outer consequences of these thoughts. Your choice lies in thinking or not thinking them in the first place. If you do not wish certain consequences to come to you, your business is to abstain from thinking them in the first place, or from thinking the kind of thoughts that will ultimate in them. If you do not want an engine to start, you do not open the valve; if you do not want a bell to ring, you do not press the button; and so, if you really understand this fundamental principle, you will from now onwards watch your habitual thinking with the utmost care.

Since it is true that the kind of thoughts that you hold in consciousness (the Secret Place) are presently going to be expressed in your outer life, in your body and affairs, you will no more think of holding inharmonious thoughts than you would think of eating or drinking something which was certain to make you very ill. Remember that whatever the mind dwells upon will sooner or later come into your experience. It does not at all follow that the particular thing you were thinking will be exactly what will happen—although sometimes it does. For instance, if you think very much about disease, you are tending to undermine your health; if you think much about poverty and depression, you are tending to bring poverty upon yourself; and if you think about trouble, and strife, and dishonesty, you attract those. The actual thing that occurs in any given instance will not commonly be the precise reproduction of any particular train of thought, but rather the resultant of the combined action of that train of thought and of your general mental attitude.

Thinking about sickness or disease is only one of the two factors that produce bodily ailments, and it is usually the less important. The other, and more important factor, is the entertainment of negative or destructive emotions, although this fact seems to be very little understood, even among students of metaphysics. So important is it, however, that it is simply impossible to insist too strongly upon the fact that most bodily ailments are caused by the patient's allowing destructive emotions to hold a place in his mind. It cannot be too often repeated that to entertain feelings of anger, resentment, jealousy, spite, and so forth, is certain to damage your health in some way or other, and quite likely to damage it very severely indeed. Remember that the question of the justification or otherwise for such feelings does not arise at all. It has absolutely nothing to do with the results, for the thing is a matter of natural law.

A woman said: "I have a right to be angry," meaning that she had been the victim of very shabby treatment, and that she consequently possessed a kind of license or special permit to hold angry feelings without their natural consequences upon the body following. This, of course, is absurd. There is no one to give such a permit, and if it could be done—if general laws could ever be set aside in special instances—we should have, not a universe, but a chaos. If you press the button, from no matter what motive, good or bad—to save a man's life or to murder him—the electric bell will ring; because that is the law of electricity. If you drank a deadly poison inadvertently, you would die or at least seriously damage your body, because such is the law. You may have mistakenly supposed it to be a harmless fluid, but that would make no difference because the law takes no account of intentions. For the same reason, to entertain negative emotions is to order trouble—primarily physical trouble, and also trouble in general—quite independently of any seeming justification which you may suppose yourself to have.

I once came across an old sermon which was delivered in London during the French Revolution. The author, who took an extremely superficial view of the Gospel, said, referring to the Sermon on the Mount: "Surely it is justifiable to hate the Arch-Butcher, Robespierre, and to execrate the Bristol murderer." This pronouncement perfectly illustrates the fallacy which we have been considering. To entertain hatred is *ipso facto* to involve yourself in certain unpleasant results and, as far as you are concerned, it will not make the faintest shadow of difference whether you are attaching the label "Robespierre," or "Tom," or "Dick," or "Harry," to the emotion concerned. The question whether the man Robespierre was, in fact, a demon or an angel of light, has nothing whatever to do with the matter.

To indulge in a sense of execration of anyone (quite irrespective of any question of deserts, or otherwise, in the object of your condemnation) is certain to bring trouble upon your own head proportionate to the intensity of the feeling you entertain, and the number of times or minutes that you devote to it. No Scientific Christian ever considers hatred or execration to be "justifiable" in any circumstances, but whatever your opinion about that may be, there is no question about its practical consequences to you. You might just as well swallow a dose of prussic acid in two gulps, and think to protect yourself by saying, "This one is for Robespierre; and this one for the Bristol murderer." You will hardly have any doubt as to who will receive the benefit of the poison.

It is very significant that Jesus should call your consciousness the "Secret Place." He desires, as always, to impress us with the truth that it is the inner that causes the outer, and not the outer that brings about the condition of the inner. Neither does one outer thing ever cause another outer thing. Cause and effect are from the within to the without. This all-embracing Master Law is not difficult to grasp in theory once it has been clearly enunciated. In practice, however, it is extraordinarily difficult to avoid losing sight of it in the rush and tumble of everyday life. We are so constituted that we can give our conscious attention to only one thing at a time, and when we are not deliberately attending to the observance of this law, when the interest in what we are doing or saying monopolizes our attention, our already-formed thought-habits are sure to determine the tenor of our thinking. We constantly forget the Master Law in practice until we have drilled ourselves into its observance with the utmost care. Meanwhile, as long as we go on breaking the law, even though it be in forgetfulness, we shall continue to incur punishment.

It is obvious from this that nothing is worthwhile, nothing has any real significance, but a change of policy in the Secret Place. Think rightly, and sooner or later all will be well on the outside. Rest content with change in the outer observance without also changing your thoughts and feelings, and you not only waste your time, but you may easily lull yourself into a false sense of security, and live in a fool's paradise. You are also extremely likely to fall into the sin of hypocrisy.

From time immemorial mankind has cherished the pathetic illusion that outward acts, which are so easy, can be made to take the place of an interior change in thought and feeling, which is so difficult. It is so easy to buy and wear ceremonial garments, to repeat set prayers by rote at certain times, to use stereotyped forms of devotion, to attend religious services at prescribed periods—and to leave the heart unchanged. The phylacteries of the Pharisees took but a moment to fasten on; but the cleansing of the heart takes hours and years of earnest prayer and self-discipline. A distinguished Quaker some years ago said: "In my youth we discontinued the distinctive Quaker costume and certain other usages, because we realized that people who were far from really caring for our Quaker ideals were joining us, nevertheless, for the sake of the educational facilities they could obtain so inexpensively for their children, as well as other advantages of our membership. It was so easy to style oneself a 'Friend,' to purchase and wear a coat without buttons or collar, and to interlard the conversation with a grammatical peculiarity, while leaving the character completely untouched."

The Quakers are not the only people who have had to meet this problem. This danger was really the rock upon which Puritanism was ultimately wrecked. The Puritans came at last to insist upon an outer conformity in all sorts of inessential points, attaching civil and sometimes criminal penalties to their neglect. Even in matters to which no statute can well be applied, it came to be understood that a certain deportment, a style in dressing, the liberal use of an artificial phraseology, such practices as saddling one's children with outlandish Old Testament names, would be so many passports to preferment in civil, ecclesiastical and often commercial life—as though such trifles could have any spiritual value in themselves, and were not, in reality, merely the simplest way of making an easy path for spiritual pride and blatant hypocrisy. It is unquestionable that the spiritualization of thought does, in practice, undoubtedly lead the student to simplify his mode of life, for so many things that previously seemed important are now found to be unimportant and uninteresting. It is unquestionable too, that he gradually finds himself meeting different people, reading different books, spending his time differently; and that his conversation naturally changes its quality too. "Old things are passed away." "Behold I make all things new." These things follow upon the change of heart; never can they precede it.

Now we see how vain is the foolish attempt to acquire popularity, or to cultivate the good opinion of other people under the impression that such a thing can be of any real advantage to us. Those who listened to the Sermon on the Mount had often seen the baser elements among the Pharisees performing good works in the most ostentatious way, in order to win the reputation of being exceptionally orthodox and saintly, and probably with a muddled impression that they were actually advancing their spiritual welfare as well. Jesus has analyzed and exposed that kind of fallacy once and for all in this section. He says that the applause that follows upon outer acts is the only reward they ever bring, and that results worthwhile are only to be obtained in the Secret Place of Consciousness where, if we pray (scientifically) to our Father in secret, He will reward us openly with a genuine demonstration.

Jesus here also lays stress upon the need for keeping our prayers "alive." Merely to repeat a phrase mechanically as a parrot does (vain repetitions) is of no use at all. When praying, one should be constantly "feeling out," making himself receptive (not negative but *receptive*) to Divine inspiration. There is no objection to repeating a helpful phrase constantly, even without any realization at all, provided it does not become mechanical; Jesus himself repeated his words three times at the moment of his dire need in the garden (*Matt.* 26:44). If ever you feel that you are getting "waterlogged" in your prayers, stop, go away and do something else, and return later on with a fresh mind.

Your Father knoweth what things ye have need of, before ye ask him. We do not have to create good, for it already exists eternally in the fact of the Omnipresence of God. Nevertheless, we have to bring it into manifestation through our own personal realization of Truth. This text does not mean that we are not to pray concerning particular needs or particular problems. Some people have interpreted it in the sense that we should work only for general harmony, but this is incorrect. If you treat only for general harmony, the results of your work will be spread over every department of your life, and the improvement in any particular detail may be so small as to be negligible. The proper course is to concentrate your prayers upon whatever you wish to demonstrate at the moment.

We do not pray for a thing as an object in itself, it is true; but when we experience a lack, whether, let us say, it be money, or a position, or a house, or a friend, we treat ourselves—the soul—concerning that sense of lack, and, when we have prayed enough to correct our understanding upon that point, the thing we are needing will appear as a proof that the work has been done. Satisfy the sense of lack within yourself with a sense of Divine Love, and the missing thing will appear in your life of its own accord. When you say your prayers, never be afraid of being too definite, precise, and businesslike. Jesus himself was all these things. No one was ever less vague or indefinite than he was.

After this manner therefore pray ye: Our Father which art in heaven, Hallowed be thy name.

Thy kingdom come. Thy will be done in earth, as it is in heaven.

Give us this day our daily bread.

And forgive us our debts, as we forgive our debtors.

And lead us not into temptation, but deliver us from evil: For thine is the kingdom, and the power, and the glory, for ever. Amen.

For if ye forgive men their trespasses, your heavenly Father will forgive you:

But if ye forgive not men their trespasses, neither will your Father forgive your trespasses.

—MATTHEW VI

This greatest of all prayers, which we commonly call the Lord's Prayer, is, in fact, a superb summing up of the whole Jesus Christ teaching, in a form unequaled for brevity and completeness. It is really nothing less than a complete outline of Christian metaphysics, and, as the author of this book has already dealt with it at considerable length in a brochure entitled "The Lord's Prayer," there is no need to cover the same ground again here.

Suffice it to say that in these few verses it defines the nature of God and of man, and explains the true relationship between them, tells us what the universe really is, and provides a method of rapid spiritual development for those who use it intelligently every day.

Note particularly how strongly Jesus insists upon the need for forgiveness if we are to make any spiritual progress at all.

> *Moreover when ye fast, be not, as the hypocrites, of a sad countenance: for they disfigure their faces, that they may appear unto men to fast. Verily I say unto you, They have their reward.*
>
> *But thou, when thou fastest, anoint thine head, and wash thy face; That thou appear not unto men to fast, but unto thy Father which is in secret: and thy Father, which seeth in secret, shall reward thee openly.*
>
> —MATTHEW VI

Fasting was the general custom among the people in those days, and Jesus takes the practice for granted.

Fasting, as we understand it in Scientific Christianity, is the abstention from certain thoughts, chiefly negative or error thoughts, of course; but in some cases it is necessary, if you want a demonstration, to abstain for a time from thinking about a particular problem at all. There are certain problems, usually those that you have been mulling over too much, that go out or are overcome "only by prayer and fasting." In such a case it is best to give the problem a definite and final treatment, and then to leave it alone, for a time; or else hand it over bodily to someone else to handle for you, after which you keep your thoughts completely away from it.

Physical fasting has occasionally been found helpful in the overcoming of a problem, especially what is called a "chronic" difficulty, when accompanied, of course, by a spiritual treatment. This is chiefly owing to the high degree of concentration that goes with a physical fast.

Note that verse 18 is substantially a repetition of verse 6. When the Bible repeats itself in this manner, it is an indication that a point of prime importance is being dealt with.

Lay not up for yourselves treasures upon earth, where moth and rust doth corrupt, and where thieves break through and steal:

But lay up for yourselves treasures in heaven, where neither moth nor rust doth corrupt, and where thieves do not break through nor steal:

For where your treasure is, there will your heart be also.

The light of the body is the eye: if therefore thine eye be single, thy whole body shall be full of light.

But if thine eye be evil, thy whole body shall be full of darkness. If therefore the light that is in thee be darkness, how great is that darkness!

—MATTHEW VI

Having dwelt upon the nature of the Secret Place, and given Prayer, or Divine Realization, as the Key of Life, Jesus goes on to stress certain consequences that follow upon all this, with the object of showing us how we must, as speedily as possible, recast our whole lives in accordance with the new basis. For example, now that we understand that the material plane is only *objectified thought,* we should realize the folly of collecting or trying to collect large sums of money or goods, or material property of any kind. If your consciousness is right, that is, if you have a good understanding of God as the loving Source of your boundless supply, you will always be able to demonstrate whatever money or goods you may require, wherever you are, or whatever your conditions may be. You cannot want for anything when once you truly realize that in Divine Mind demand and supply are one. And, on the contrary, until you do realize this, you never will be really safe from want. You may, indeed, acquire a very large share of the world's goods in the way of bank balance, stocks and bonds, real estate, or whatnot; but unless you have attained enough spiritual understanding, these things are more likely than not sooner or later to take unto themselves wings and fly away. In fact, there is no way in which one can have security without spiritual understanding.

The "safest" banks can and do fail; unforeseen catastrophes happen on the stock market; mines and oil wells give out or may be destroyed by some natural cataclysm; a new invention may easily ruin an old one, the opening or closing of a railroad station, or the starting of some new enterprise somewhere else, may ruin the value of your real estate; to say nothing of the unpredictable effect of unexpected political upheavals upon every kind of property. In short, it is waste of time to give too much attention to collecting material possessions which are so vulnerable to changes and chances, to "moth and rust," and thieves.

If a reasonable part of the time and attention that most people spend in the pursuit of material goods were devoted by them to scientific prayer and meditation, the change in consciousness which would follow would put them beyond any possibility of suffering from any of these hazards.

If you had sufficient spiritual understanding of supply, your investments probably would not go wrong; but if they did, your losses would be immediately replaced in some other way, and before you had time to suffer from them. If, let us say, the bank in which your fortune was deposited should stop payment on Monday, then, probably before the end of the week, an equivalent sum of money, or at least as much as you could possibly need, would come to you from somewhere else—if you had sufficient spiritual understanding. If any case, the owner of a prosperity consciousness cannot be impoverished; nor, for the matter of that, can the owner of a poverty consciousness be permanently enriched.

In the long run, no one can retain what does not belong to him by right of consciousness, nor be deprived of that which is truly his by the same supreme title.

Therefore, you will do well not to lay up to yourself treasures upon earth, but rather to lay up treasure in heaven; that is, the understanding of Spiritual Law. If you are looking to outer, passing, mutable things for either happiness or security, you are not putting God first. If you are putting God first in your life, you will not find yourself laboring under undue anxiety about anything, for *where your treasure is, there will your heart be also.*

Pursuing the same train of ideas in greater detail, Jesus goes on to say that those who are upon the new basis are to be free from all sorts of petty anxieties and worrying details which continue to afflict those who are not. Questions of diet, for instance, will settle themselves if one is thinking rightly. A follower of the new life does not need to watch every bite that he puts into his mouth, until eating becomes a burden. He eats naturally and spontaneously of the ordinary food that comes along, knowing that his habitual right thought will take care of his diet too. If he had been accustomed to eating more than was good for him, the fact that he now prays every day for wisdom and guidance in general would lead to his eating less; or, if he should not be eating enough, then scientific daily prayer would cause him to eat more until the right quantity was reached.

The same principle applies to all the details of everyday living. If you pray for yourself in the right way every day, you will find that the minor things of life will gradually fall correctly into place of their own accord without any trouble on your part. Contrast this with the usual method of trying to get everything right by separately organizing a thousand petty details, and you will appreciate how wonderfully the new spiritual basis sets you free. *If thine eye be single, thy whole body shall be full of light.* This is the summation of all Truth. Verily, if the *eye be single,* the *whole body* of experience *shall be full of light.*

The eye symbolizes spiritual perception. *Whatever you give your attention to, is the thing that governs your life.* Attention is the key. Your free will lies in the directing of your attention. Whatever you steadfastly direct your attention to, will come into your life and dominate it. If you do not direct your attention consistently to anything in particular—and many people do not—then nothing in particular will come into your life except uncertainty and suspense; you will be like a drifting log. If you direct your attention to the outer world of manifestation, which is in its nature continually shifting and changing, you are bound to have unhappiness, poverty, and ill-health; whereas, if you direct your attention to God; if the Glory of God comes first with you, and to express His Will becomes the rule of your life, then your eye is single and your whole body, or embodiment, will be full of light.

No man can serve two masters: for either he will hate the one, and love the other; or else he will hold to the one, and despise the other. Ye cannot serve God and mammon.

Therefore I say unto you, Take no thought for your life, what ye shall eat, or what ye shall drink; nor yet for your body, what ye shall put on. Is not the life more than meat, and the body than raiment?

Behold the fowls of the air: for they sow not, neither do they reap, nor gather into barns; yet your heavenly Father feedeth them. Are ye not much better than they?

Which of you by taking thought can add one cubit unto his stature?

And why take ye thought for raiment? Consider the lilies of the field, how they grow; they toil not, neither do they spin:

And yet I say unto you, That even Solomon in all his glory was not arrayed like one of these.

Wherefore, if God so clothe the grass of the field, which today is, and tomorrow is cast into the oven, shall he not much more clothe you, O ye of little faith?

Therefore take no thought, saying, What shall we eat? or, What shall we drink? or, Wherewithal shall we be clothed?

(For after all these things do the Gentiles seek:) for your heavenly Father knoweth that ye have need of all these things.

But seek ye first the kingdom of God, and his righteousness; and all these things shall be added unto you.

—MATTHEW VI

Many Christians have accepted these facts theoretically, but have been less than half-hearted when it came to their practical application, and this vacillation has landed them in the mass of difficulties that always follow upon inconsistency and weakness. It is found that those who are altogether upon the material basis have, on the whole, a better time, for they are at least living in accordance with the best that they know, and playing the game as they understand it. To try to rest sometimes upon one basis, and sometimes upon the other, is to try to *serve two masters*. And this of course cannot be done. *Ye cannot serve God and mammon.*

Man is essentially spiritual, the image and likeness of God, and therefore he is made for the Spiritual Basis, and he cannot really succeed on any other. The birds of the air and the lilies of the field furnish a striking lesson to man in their complete adaptation to the laws of their own respective planes. They thoroughly express their own true natures; they go through their lives perfectly themselves, and without knowing anything like the worry and anxiety that warp so many human lives. The lilies referred to are the beautiful wild poppies of the East, and whoever has seen a field of poppies dancing and swaying in the breeze will appreciate the sense of relaxation and freedom and joy that Jesus had in mind as being our true birthright.

Of course, he did not mean that you as a human being are to copy the lives or the methods of the birds or flowers literally, for you are infinitely higher in the scale of creation than they are. The lesson is that you are to adapt yourself as completely to your element as they do to theirs. Your true element is the Presence of God. Augustine said: "Thou hast made us for Thyself, and our hearts are restless until they repose in Thee." When man accepts the Truth that in God he lives and moves and has his being, as completely and un-questioningly as the birds and the flowers accept the truth of *their* condition, he will demonstrate as easily and as thoroughly as they do.

If anyone were so foolish as to take these beautiful similes literally, instead of spiritually, and should, let us say, lie down in a field among the poppies waiting for God to perform a dramatic miracle on his behalf, he would speedily learn by experience that this is not the way. Possessing faculties infinitely above the vegetable or the animal kingdoms, he will truly emulate the wisdom and the glory of these by being ceaselessly active in his own realm, that of prayer and meditation. The Spiritual Basis does not mean *laissez faire;* it means intensified activity, but on the spiritual as distinct from the material plane. This is the only way in which one can be said to be seeking first the Kingdom of Heaven; and all needful things will be found to follow upon that.

If you are very worried and confused or very much discouraged, that is the time to lie down among the poppies mentally, and read the Bible or pray gently but persistently until something happens; either something within yourself or something in the outer picture. This is not *laissez faire,* because you are praying. A woman in London, whose affairs seemed to have got into a hopeless tangle that meant utter ruin, was persuaded by me to drop the whole burden mentally and "let the worst happen," while she spent two or three days browsing through the Bible and praying for peace and happiness. Everything cleared up like magic within a week without her having taken any material action.

The normal mode of obtaining one's supply is by following some useful business or profession in which one should be happy and satisfied, doing good work and receiving a liberal compensation for it. Scientific prayer will put anyone into such a position if he does not already possess it, and then if he prays each day as he should, realizing true place, and claiming opportunities for service, his actual position, whatever it is, will be continually improving as time goes on. Of course this does not mean that one need necessarily "go out to business," as it is called. The woman taking care of her household duties at home is just as useful a citizen as anyone in the land; and many people whose private incomes put them beyond the need of earning money, lead lives of the highest usefulness in developing literature and art, and in other activities. What is certain is that no one upon the Spiritual Basis will lead the life of an idler, however much money he may have.

One hears occasionally of curious cases of people who claim to be so spiritual that they do not feel called upon to earn their own living. Someone else, a relative, or friend, who is not too spiritual to go to work, is expected to keep them in idleness. But this attitude of mind speaks for itself. If your understanding of metaphysics is sufficient to enable you to dispense with ordinary work, you will find yourself automatically supplied, and in an independent and self-respecting manner, with a good living. This cannot possibly apply to people who are in debt or sponging upon others. If you really wish to try the experiment of "stepping out" upon the power of the Word, by all means do so; but be sure that your so doing is authentic. The only way to make this experiment in a genuine manner is to let it be "demonstrate or starve." If you are secretly looking to someone else to come to the rescue, you are not really depending upon the Word. Every Scientific Christian is entitled to reasonable prosperity, which means enough to live on in decent comfort and reasonable security. Until you can demonstrate this genuinely by the power of the Word alone, you should use your treatment to find a position and to make it a success.

Jesus tells us in this section that by taking thought we cannot add one cubit to our stature. This is one more way of stating the great truth that he states in so many ways; namely, that we have to be born again. As long as you remain the man that you are, you cannot by merely taking thought be or do anything except what you are (because, of course, you always do what you are); you can only "get anywhere," as they say, by becoming a different man, and this you can only do by getting some realization of the Presence of God.

Take therefore no thought for the morrow: for the morrow shall take thought for the things of itself.

Sufficient unto the day is the evil thereof.

—MATTHEW VI

In scientific prayer we usually work in the present tense. The whole idea of scientific prayer is to adjust one's consciousness, and this must necessarily be done in the present— "Behold now is the accepted time. Behold now is the day of salvation." When a problem concerning your future presents itself to you—for example, suppose that you have to sit for an examination in six months' time, or to take a voyage which you dread, perhaps next week—the right thing is to pray about it now, in the present tense. Do not wait until the time comes, but work on it now; that is, work on your own consciousness concerning it, and in the present tense. Do not try, as it were, to throw your treatment forward. This cannot be done successfully. The event may be a future one, but the very fact that you are thinking of it at all means that it is present in consciousness; and as the thought is a present one, it can and must be dealt with in the present tense. In the same way you can treat about past events, and you should do so if they still worry you, by treating about them in the present tense—because the thought of them is present. Treat for past and future events alike as though the incident were going on at the present moment. Remember that God is outside of what we call time, and the beautiful healing action of His Holy Presence is just as applicable to one date as to another.

Always remember that the only thought that you need to concern yourself with is the present one. The thoughts of yesterday or of last year do not matter now, because if you can get the present thought right it will make everything else right here and now. The best way to prepare for tomorrow is to make today's consciousness serene and harmonious. All other good things will follow upon that.

Never go delving into your mind to look for troubles to pray or treat about. Deal faithfully with those that bring themselves to your attention, and hidden things will be taken care of.

In the same spirit, Scientific Christianity discourages too much consideration of the next plane, and of afterdeath conditions. Such preoccupations are too often but a flight from the realities of this life and of everyday problems that should be faced and solved here—not evaded or, what is the same thing, postponed in thought.

We are to dwell upon Life, and not death, and to concentrate upon making our demonstration here and now.

CHAPTER SIX

WITH WHAT
MEASURE YE METE

Judge not, that ye be not judged.

For with what judgment ye judge, ye shall be judged: and with what measure ye mete, it shall be measured to you again.

And why beholdest thou the mote that is in thy brother's eye, but considerest not the beam that is in thine own eye?

Or how will thou say to thy brother, Let me pull out the mote out of thine eye; and, behold, a beam is in thine own eye?

Thou hypocrite, first cast out the beam out of thine own eye; and then shalt thou see clearly to cast out the mote out of thy brother's eye.

—MATTHEW VII

This section of the Sermon on the Mount consists of five short verses, and only about one hundred words, and yet it is hardly too much to say that at its simple face value it is the most staggering document ever presented to mankind. In these five verses we are told more about the nature of man and the meaning of life, and the importance of conduct, and the art of living, and the secret of happiness and success, and the way out of trouble, and the approach to God, and the emancipation of the soul, and the salvation of the world, than all the philosophers and the theologians and the savants put together have told us—for it explains the Great Law. It is vastly more important that a man, and still more that a child, should be taught the meaning of these five verses than that he should learn anything else that is taught in schools or colleges. There is nothing to be found in any of the ordinary courses of study; there is nothing to be learned in any library, or in any laboratory that is one-millionth part as important as the information contained herein. If it were ever possible to justify the fanatical saying "Burn the rest of the books, for it is all in this one," it would be in reference to those words.

Judge not that ye be not judged. For with what judgment ye judge, ye shall be judged; and with what measure ye mete, it shall be measured to you again. If the average man understood for a single moment the meaning of these words, and really believed them to be true, they would immediately revolutionize his whole life from top to bottom; turn his everyday conduct inside out, and so change him that, in a comparatively short space of time, his closest friends would hardly know him. Whether he were the Prime Minister in the Cabinet or the man in the street, this understanding would turn the world upside down for him, and, because the thing is infectious beyond computing, it would turn the world upside down for many, many others as well.

Again and again we are struck with amazement, upon rereading this Sermon on the Mount with a fresh mind, to find how completely its most challenging statements have been quietly ignored in practice by the bulk of the Christian world. If one did not know for a fact that these words are constantly heard in public, and read in private, by millions and millions of Christians of all sorts, he could hardly believe it to be possible; for the truths which they teach seem to be the last consideration to enter into people's motives in everyday life and conduct—and yet they express the simple and inescapable Law of Life.

The plain fact is that it is the Law of Life that, as we think, and speak, and act towards others, so will others think, and speak, and act towards us. Whatever sort of conduct we give out, that we are inevitably bound to get back. Anything and everything that we do to others will sooner or later be done to us by someone, somewhere. The good that we do to others we shall receive back in like measure; and the evil that we do to others in like manner we shall receive back too. This does not in the least mean that the same people whom we treat well or ill will be the actual ones to return the action. That almost never happens; but what does happen is that at some other time or place, often far away and long afterwards, someone else who knows nothing whatever of the previous action will, nevertheless, repay it, grain for grain, to us. For every unkind word that you speak to or about another person, an unkind word will be spoken to or about you. For every time that you cheat, you will be cheated. For every time that you deceive you will be deceived. For every lie that you utter, you will be lied to. Every time that you neglect a duty, or evade a responsibility, or misuse authority over other people, you are doing something for which you will inevitably have to pay by suffering a like injury yourself. *With what measure ye mete, it shall be measured to you again.*

Now, is it not obvious that if only people realized all this as being literally true, it would have the profoundest influence on their conduct? Would not such an understanding do more in practice to decrease crime and raise the general moral standard of the community than all the laws ever passed by parliaments, or all the formal punishments meted out by judges and magistrates? People are very apt to think, especially when they are strongly tempted, that they can probably escape the law of the land, outrun the constable, or slip through the clutches of authority in some other way. They hope that individuals will forgive them, or else be powerless to revenge their actions; or that the thing will be forgotten sometime; or, better still, that they will never be found out at all. If, however, they understood that the law of retribution is a Cosmic Law, impersonal and unchanging as the law of gravity; neither considering persons nor respecting institutions; without rancor but without pity; they would think twice before they treated other people unjustly. The law of gravity never sleeps, is never off duty or off its guard, is never tired out, is neither compassionate nor vindictive; and no one would ever dream of trying to evade it, or coax it, or bribe it, or intimidate it. People accept it as being inevitable and inescapable, and they shape their conduct accordingly—and the law of retribution is even as the law of gravity. Water finds its own level sooner or later and our treatment of others returns at last upon ourselves.

Some Christian people, upon hearing the law of retribution explained, have objected that this is Buddhism or Hinduism, and not Christianity. Now it is perfectly true that this law is taught by the Buddhists, and by the Hinduists, and wisely so—because it is the law of nature. It is also true that the law is better understood in Oriental countries than among us; but this does not make it an Oriental possession. It simply means that the orthodox Christian churches have largely neglected to make an important section of the Christian teaching clear to the people.

To those who say that it is un-Christian, I reply with a question: Is the Gospel of Matthew a Christian document, or not? Was Jesus Christ a Christian or a Buddhist? You may like or dislike the doctrine, and if you wish, you may try to ignore it; but you cannot deny that Jesus Christ taught it, and in the most direct and emphatic way when he said: *Judge not that ye be not judged. For with what judgment ye judge, ye shall be judged; and with what measure ye mete, it shall be measured to you again.*

A beautiful description of the Law has been written for English-speaking people by Sir Edwin Arnold in *The Song Celestial:*

> *It will not be contemned of any one;*
> *Who thwarts it loses, and who serves it gains;*
> *The hidden good it pays with peace and bliss,*
> *The hidden ill with pains.*
> *By this the slayer's knife did stab himself;*
> *The unjust judge hath lost his own defender;*
> *The false tongue dooms its lie; the creeping thief*
> *And spoiler rob, to render.*
> *It seeth everywhere and marketh all:*
> *Do right—it recompenseth! do one wrong—*
> *The equal retribution must be made,*
> *Though Dharma tarry long.*

Now we see that we had better not do to anyone else anything that we do not wish to have done to us, because that is what will happen. Particularly is this the case if we act badly towards someone who is in our power.

But it is a poor law that does not work both ways, and so it is equally true that for every good deed that you do, for every kind word that you speak, you will in the same way, at some time or other, get back an equivalent. People often complain of ingratitude on the part of those on whom they have conferred favors, and too often with truth; but this complaint shows a false attitude of mind which it is important to correct. When you feel hurt because someone has been ungrateful for your kindness, it shows that you have been looking for gratitude, and this is a great mistake. The true reason for helping another is that it is our duty to help others insofar as we can do so wisely; or because it is an expression of love. Of course, love will not look for a *quid pro quo,* and to have done one's duty should be its own reward, remembering, if we wish, that in some other way the deed will surely be recognized. The very fact that one is looking for gratitude means that he is putting the other person under a sense of obligation, and that person will probably get this subconsciously and resent it strongly, as such a thing is highly repugnant to human nature. Do your good deed, and then pass on, neither expecting nor wishing for personal recognition.

Is it not a beautiful and encouraging thought that all the prayers you have ever said in your life, and all the good deeds and kind words for which you have ever been responsible are still with you, and that nothing can ever take them away? Indeed, our prayers and our words and acts of kindness to others are the only things that we do keep, for all the rest must disappear. Errors of thought, word, and deed are worked out and satisfied under the Law, but the good goes on forever, unchanged and undimmed by time.

Students of Scientific Christianity who understand the power of thought, will realize that it is here, in the realm of thought, that the Law finds its true application; and they will see that the one thing that matters, in the last resort, is to keep their thoughts right about other people—even as about themselves. The right thought about God, and the right thought about fellow man, and the right thought about one's self; that is the Law and the Prophets. Knowing that Dominion is located in the Secret Place, it is on the Secret Place that they will focus their attention in observing the commandment—*judge not.*

The Golden Rule in Scientific Christianity is: *Think about others as you would wish them to think about you.* In the light of the knowledge that we now possess, the observance of this rule becomes a very solemn duty, but, more than that indeed, it is a vital debt of honor. A debt of honor is an obligation that cannot be enforced at law, but depends for its discharge upon the honor and self-respect of the debtor, and, in like manner, since no one can know or prove how we are thinking, we are not responsible for our thoughts to any tribunal but the highest one of all—the Tribunal which never makes mistakes, and whose decisions are never evaded.

The student having now gained an understanding of what the Great Law is and how it works, as it is so wonderfully summed up by Jesus in this section, is in a position to take the next great step and understand how *it is possible to rise above even the Great Law itself, in the name of* THE CHRIST. In the Bible the term "Christ" is not identical with Jesus, the individual. It is a technical term which may be briefly defined as the Absolute Spiritual Truth about anything. Now, to know this Truth about any person, or condition, or circumstance, immediately heals that person, or condition, or circumstance, to the extent that such Truth is realized by the thinker. This is the essence of spiritual healing, and thus we see that in the widest sense, and altogether independently of the special and unparalleled work that was done for us by Jesus himself, it is true that the Christ comes into the world to redeem it and save it. Whenever the Christ (that is, the True Idea concerning anything) is raised up in thought by anyone, healing follows—physical healing, or moral healing, or even intellectual healing, as the case may be.

Intellectual healing would be to make a dull or stupid person bright and intelligent. Backward school children respond like magic to such treatment. One should claim Divine Intelligence for them and realize that God is the soul of man. Sickness and sin, poverty and confusion, weakness of character, all disappear under the power of the Healing Christ. It makes no difference how deeply seated may be the trouble, the realization by somebody of the Christ, or the Spiritual Truth behind the appearance, will heal it. There is no exception whatever to this. Because the Christ is nothing less than the direct action of God Himself, the Self-knowing of Spirit, it overrides all else.

The higher law of Spirit overrides or supersedes all the lower laws of the physical and mental planes. This, as we saw in the first chapter, does not mean that the laws of the physical or mental planes are broken. It means that man, because of his essential Divine Selfhood, has the power of rising above these domains into the infinite dimension of Spirit where such laws no longer affect him. He has not broken their laws, but has adventured beyond them. A very inadequate simile may be cited in the case of the balloon which rushes away from the ground seemingly in defiance of the law of gravity, as soon as the bag is inflated. Here it seems as if the law of gravity were broken, but of course it is not broken, but rather, completely fulfilled by such action; yet the normal experience of ordinary life actually is reversed. Now the Law of Karma, which is no respecter of persons, and forgets nothing, is actually law for matter and mind only; it is not law for Spirit. In Spirit all is perfect and eternal, unchanging good. Here there is no bad Karma to be reaped, because none can be sown, and thus when man, by what we call prayer, meditation, or treatment, transfers his attention to the domain of Spirit, he comes—to that extent—under the law of perfect Good, and Karma is wiped out.

So man has the choice of Karma or Christ. This is the best news that has ever come to mankind, and for that reason it is called the good news, or the glad tidings, or the Gospel, for such is the meaning of this word. This is man's charter of freedom, his dominion over all things as the Image and Likeness of God. He has his choice. He can remain in the limited region of matter and mind, in which case he is bound fast on the wheel of Karma; or, he can appeal, through prayer, to the Realm of Spirit—that is, the Christ—and be free. But he has the choice—Christ or Karma; and CHRIST IS LORD OF KARMA.

In the East where Karma is so well understood, they are without the Christian message of the Christ, and they therefore find themselves in a rather hopeless position. We, however, who rightly understand the Gospel of the Christ, can be free. In other words, Karma turns out to be inexorable only so long as you do not pray. As soon as you pray, you begin to rise above Karma; that is to say, you begin to wipe out the unpleasant consequences of past mistakes. For any given mistake, you must either suffer the consequences, which we call being punished, or wipe them out by scientific prayer—the Practice of the Presence of God. You have the grand choice—Christ or Karma.

Does this mean that any mistake, any stupidity, any heinous sin even, can be expunged from the Book of Life, with all punishment or suffering naturally accruing to it? Yes, it means nothing less than that. There is no evil that the Healing Christ will not destroy. God so loves the world that he manifests His unique Christ Power, that whosoever chooses it shall not perish through his own weakness or frailty, but have everlasting salvation.

It must not, needless to say, be supposed that the consequences of a mistake are to be cheaply evaded by a perfunctory prayer. Not so indeed. No superficial prayer, but sufficient realization of God to alter fundamentally the character of the sinner, is required in order to wipe out the punishment that otherwise must always follow upon sin. When sufficient prayer or treatment has been done so that the sinner becomes a changed man, and will not even desire to repeat his sin, then is he saved; and then are the penalties remitted, for Christ is Lord of Karma.

CHAPTER SEVEN

BY THEIR
FRUITS

Give not that which is holy unto the dogs, neither cast ye your pearls before swine, lest they trample them under their feet, and turn again and rend you.

—MATTHEW VII

Intelligence is just as essential a part of the Christian message as is love. God is love, but God is also infinite intelligence, and unless these two qualities are balanced in our lives, we do not get wisdom; for *wisdom is the perfect blending of intelligence and love.* Love without intelligence may do much undesigned harm—the spoiled child is a case in point—and intelligence without love may ultimate in clever cruelty. All true Christian activity will express wisdom, for zeal without discretion is proverbially mischievous.

It often happens that when people first become possessed of a knowledge of the Truth, and are perhaps set free from some oppressing difficulty, they are so overjoyed that they go running about pouring out their discovery to others, indiscriminately; and probably urging them to accept the Truth too. It is entirely understandable that this should happen, for love longs to share its good; but, nevertheless, it is very unwise. The fact is that the acceptance of Truth involves, as we have seen, the scrapping of all the old standards; and, after all, this is a tremendous thing to expect from anyone, and it can only happen, in any case, when people are spiritually ready for the change. If one is spiritually ready, he will be glad to accept Truth, if it be put forward in some way that can appeal to him; if he be not ready, no amount of intellectual discussion or argument will make him so.

Never rely upon your own judgment to say who is ready for the Truth and who is not; but rely for guidance upon the inspiration of the Holy Spirit. Most of us have had the experience, when we first realized the Spiritual Idea and what it means, of picking out certain of our friends who, we felt sure, would jump at it, only to find that in most cases they refused to take it at all. On the other hand, several people whom we, in our foolishness, chose to regard as being unspiritual (because they did not seem to be spiritual) accepted it gladly and made a great success with it. If you are praying regularly every day for wisdom, intelligence, and fresh opportunities for service, the right people will be brought to you, or you will be brought to them; and a convenient occasion will be provided for the subject to be introduced. If, when in company with anyone, you are doubtful whether or not to broach the subject of Truth, do not; but pray for guidance instead, and leave the matter to the action of God. Sometimes nothing happens, no convenient opportunity presents itself while you are with your friend, and that means that the time is not ripe and that no good would have been done by speaking. Very often, however, an obvious opening does occur in the conversation, after the treatment has been given, or some external incident happens which furnishes an opening for introducing the subject; and I have seen some very surprising and pleasant awakenings happen in this way.

Above all things, be chary of forcing the subject of Truth upon the people with whom you have to live and work; especially in your home. It is easy to make yourself nothing less than a constant nuisance by forcing your ideas upon people who cannot appreciate them, because they are not ready. As members of your household and business associates have naturally to see a good deal of you, and you of them, such a policy will probably give rise to a good deal of friction, and even ill feeling. Try to realize that in the absence of your personal awakening they cannot possibly see the thing as you do; and that they are therefore seeing something else. Also, you may not be very skillful in expounding your ideas in the best way. Finally, remember that those with whom you associate closely will have your personal conduct under constant inspection, will be familiar with many of your faults and weaknesses, and, if you talk too much and without a good deal of wisdom concerning spiritual enlightenment, will be sure to look for a greater demonstration than you may be able to make in the beginning, and they will have to be of rather more than average humanity if they do not sometimes point out discrepancies at most unwelcome moments—if you have been too aggressive. In other words, "hasten slowly" is here the watchword. It cannot help the spread of Truth at all for you to get the reputation of being a crank or a nuisance. The quickest way to spread it is by living the life yourself. Then, people will notice the change in you, and, as they see improved health and prosperity in your life, and happiness shining in your face, they will come round of their own accord, begging to share your secret. They will require no urging to drink the waters of life.

When you are desirous of introducing the Truth to a particular person, or to a group of people, the proper course is to prepare yourself by a special daily treatment for several days, or better still for a week or two, in advance. Work for Intelligence, Love (to overcome impatience, and to help you to meet ridicule or seeming unkindness), and, above all, for Wisdom, which, as we have seen, is the right union of the other two. Claim that the action of God will make you say the right thing when the time comes, and that it will also endow your listener or listeners with the same qualities. Do not allow yourself to care in the least what the actual result of the discussion may turn out to be. Voice the Truth, and leave it. You will often be amazed at the results you will get following a few days' spiritual preparation of this kind.

Ask, and it shall be given you; seek, and ye shall find; knock, and it shall be opened unto you:

For every one that asketh receiveth; and he that seeketh findeth; and to him that knocketh it shall be opened.

Or what man is there of you, whom if his son ask bread, will he give him a stone?

Or if he ask a fish, will he give him a serpent?

If ye then, being evil, know how to give good gifts unto your
children, how much more shall your Father which is in heaven
give good things to them that ask him?

—MATTHEW VII

This is the wonderful passage in which Jesus enunciates the primary truth of the Fatherhood of God. This truth may be called primary because it is the foundation stone upon which the whole structure of true religion is built. Until men could understand the meaning of the Fatherhood of God, and something of what that implies, they could hardly obtain any satisfactory religious experience. As long as men had believed that there were many gods, a sound religious experience was not possible, for all genuine religious experience is a search for conscious union with the One. Many gods must necessarily be gods of limitation; and as they were always, and necessarily, represented as being in conflict among themselves, only chaotic thought could follow from such a belief. Those who had got beyond that idea to the concept of the One or True God, still thought of Him almost universally as a kind of Oriental tyrant-king, or sultan, owning and governing man with a rod of iron, on much the same lines that a capricious human tyrant might be expected to pursue. The God of many of the Old Testament writers is a very jealous, revengeful, and cruel despot; a sultan whom it is almost impossible to please, implacable in his anger, often indiscriminate in his vengeance. He seems to have no more in common with mankind than men have with the animals; in fact much less, for we do conceive ourselves to share many of the lowest creatures' limitations in a common susceptibility to suffering and hunger and death.

This Oriental-sultan view of God was actually the view held by very many earnest orthodox Christians down to very recent times, be it remembered, and it denied to man anything in common with God at all. A witty modern writer has compared this god to a certain English millionaire who keeps a private zoo near London as his own personal hobby. It is stocked with a number of creatures which exist solely for their owner's interest and pleasure. He visits his menagerie from time to time and (acting no doubt on expert advice) orders certain animals to be destroyed, others to be moved into more commodious cages, and others again perhaps to be dealt with in this way or that. He has, of course, no spiritual communion with them whatever. They are simply so many animated toys that exist for his entertainment. This is not by any means an overstrained description of the ideas held by many Fundamentalists, for instance.

In this passage Jesus once and for all lays the axe to the root of this horrible superstition for those who will read their Bible with an open mind. He says here, definitely and clearly—and he stresses his words in the most circumstantial way—that the real relationship of God and man is that of parent and child. Here God ceases to be the distant potentate who deals with grovelling slaves, and becomes the loving Father of us, His children. It is extremely difficult to realize the far-reaching importance that this declaration holds for the life of the soul. If you will read and reread this section dealing with the Fatherhood of God every day for a few weeks, you will find that it alone answers a great many of your religious problems. I venture to say that you will be considerably surprised at the large number of puzzling questions that it will settle once and for all. The teaching of Jesus concerning the Fatherhood of God was original and unique. In the Old Testament God is never addressed as "Father." Where references to His Fatherhood are made, He is referred to as the Father of the nation, and not of individuals. Indeed this was the reason why Jesus made the declaration of the Fatherhood of God the opening clause of what we call the "Lord's Prayer." It explains, for instance, the tremendous statement in Genesis that man is the image and likeness of God.

It is axiomatic, of course, that the offspring must be of the same nature and species as the parent; and so if God and man are indeed Father and child, man—notwithstanding all his present limitations, and despite all appearances to the contrary—must be essentially Divine too, and susceptible of infinite growth and improvement and development up the rising pathway of divinity. That is to say, as man's true nature—his spiritual character—unfolds, which means as he becomes more and more conscious of it, he will expand in spiritual consciousness until he has transcended all bounds of human imagination; onward, and yet onward still. It is in reference to this, our glorious destiny, that, as we have already seen, Jesus himself says elsewhere, quoting the older scriptures: "I have said ye are gods, and all of you sons of the Most High." He then emphasized his point by adding significantly: "And the scripture cannot be broken."

So, in this passage we are set free once and for all from the last link in the last chain that binds us to a limited and a degraded destiny. We are the children of God; and if children, then sons, and joint heirs with Jesus Christ, as Paul says; and as sons of God we are the heirs of our Father's estate, not strangers, or paid servants, much less chattel slaves. We are sons of the house and will one day enjoy our inheritance. At the present time we find ourselves full of limitations and disabilities because we are spiritually but children—minors. Children are irresponsible, lacking in wisdom and experience, and have to be kept under control lest their mistakes should entail serious consequences to themselves. But as soon as man comes of age spiritually, then, as we have seen above, he claims his rights and obtains them. "The heir as long as he is a child differeth nothing from a servant, though he be Lord of all, but is under tutors and governors"; but when the fullness of time is come, he awakens to the Truth, and obtains his spiritual majority. He realizes that it is the Voice of God Himself that is in his heart, making him cry: "Abba, Father." Then at last he knows that he is the son of a great King, and that all that his Father has is his for the using, whether it be health, or supply, or opportunity, or beauty, or joy, or any other of the thoughts of God.

The most mischievous thing in life is man's slowness, indeed we can say his reluctance, to perceive his own dominion. God has given us dominion over all things, but we shrink like frightened children from assuming it, although that assuming is the one and only escape for us. Mankind is often like a fugitive who sits in the driving seat of an automobile which is all ready to bear him away to safety, but who cannot bring himself, for nervousness, to grasp the controls and start the car. He sits there half-frozen with terror, glancing over his shoulder, wondering whether his pursuers will catch up with him, and what will happen to him if they do. He could make his escape into safety at any moment, but he will not, or dare not.

Jesus, who knew the human heart as no other has ever known it before or since, understood our difficulty and our weakness in this respect; and with his unparalleled magic of living words, his power of putting fundamental truth in such simple, direct, and pointed fashion that even a child could not miss it, commands us: *Ask, and it shall be given you;*

seek, and ye shall find; knock, and it shall be opened unto you; for every one that asketh receiveth; and he that seeketh findeth; and to him that knocketh it shall be opened.

It is impossible to imagine the thing being stated more definitely and compellingly than in these words. There are simply no words in any language which could be clearer or more emphatic, and yet, for the most part, Christians quietly ignore them, or else discount their meaning until they are left without any meaning at all. Now, as I have previously pointed out, we are obliged to believe either that Jesus meant what he said, or that he did not; and, as we can hardly believe that he did not, or that he could talk nonsense through want of understanding, we are compelled to accept these words as being true—and, indeed, where is there room for evasion?

Ask and ye shall receive. Is not this the Magna Charta of personal freedom for every man, woman, and child on earth? Is not this the decree of the emancipation of the slaves of every kind of bondage, physical, mental, or spiritual? What room does this leave for the so-called Christian virtue of resignation, so often preached? The fact is, of course, that resignation is not a virtue at all. On the contrary, resignation is a sin. What we commonly dignify with the fine name of resignation is really an unwholesome mixture of cowardice and sloth. We have no business to be resigned to inharmony of any kind, because inharmony cannot be the Will of God. We have no business to accept ill-health, or poverty, or sinfulness, or strife, or unhappiness, or remorse, with resignation. We have no right to accept anything less than freedom and harmony and joy, for only with these things do we glorify God, and express His Holy Will, which is our *raison d'être*.

It is our most sacred duty, out of loyalty to God Himself, to refuse to accept anything less than all-round happiness and success, and we shall not be following out the wishes and instructions of Jesus if we do accept less. We are to pray and meditate, and reorganize our lives in accordance with his teaching, continuously and untiringly until our goal is attained. That this attainment, that our victory over every negative condition, is not merely possible but is definitely promised to us, finds its proof in these glorious words, the ensign of freedom for mankind: *Ask, and ye shall receive; seek, and ye shall find; knock, and it shall be opened unto you.*

> *Therefore all things whatsoever ye would that men should do to you, do ye even so to them: for this is the law and the prophets.*
> —MATTHEW VII

This is the sublime precept that we call the Golden Rule. Here Jesus reiterates the Great Law in a concise summing up. This repetition follows upon his wonderful statement of the Fatherhood of God. The underlying explanation for the existence of the Great Law is the metaphysical fact that we are all fundamentally one—all parts of the Great Mind. Because we are all ultimately one, to hurt another is really to hurt oneself, and to help another is really to help oneself. The Fatherhood of God compels us to accept the brotherhood of man, and, spiritually, brotherhood is unity.

The understanding of this great truth includes within itself all other religious knowledge, and is, in the old phraseology, *law and the prophets.*

> *Enter ye in at the strait gate: for wide is the gate, and broad is the way, that leadeth to destruction, and many there be which go in thereat:*
>
> *Because strait is the gate, and narrow is the way, which leadeth unto life, and few there be that find it.*
> —MATTHEW VII

There is only one way under the sun by which man can attain harmony, that is to say, health, prosperity, peace of mind—salvation, in the true sense of the word—and that is by bringing about a radical and permanent change for the better in his own consciousness. This is the one and only way; there is no other. For countless generations humanity has been trying in every other conceivable way to compass its own good. Innumerable schemes have been designed to bring about happiness by making changes of some sort in man's external conditions while leaving the quality of his mentality untouched; and always the result has been the same—failure. We are now in a position to see why this must be so, that it is because the very nature of our being is such that it is only by a change in consciousness that outer conditions can really be altered. This change in consciousness is the *strait gate* that Jesus speaks of here, and, as he says, the number of those who find it is comparatively small. Today that number is increasing with great rapidity, though indeed it is still comparatively small, but at the time that Jesus spoke it was very much smaller still.

This doctrine that what matters is one's consciousness, because your own concept is what you see, Jesus calls the Way of Life, and he says that all other doctrines are but a broad road to destruction or disappointment. Now why should man be so reluctant, apparently, to try to change his consciousness? Why is it that he seems to prefer to try almost any other method however arduous or even farfetched it may be? All through history every other conceivable way has been tried to bring about the salvation of humanity, and, of course, all have failed, as we now know that they must; and yet man will seldom try the "strait" way until he is driven to it, individually, by irresistible pressure.

The answer is that, as we have already seen, the changing

of one's consciousness is really very hard work, calling for constant unceasing vigilance and a breaking of mental habits which is sure to be very troublesome for a time. The natural man is lazy, always tends to take the line of least resistance, and so, in this as in lesser matters, he does not get down to bedrock principles until he is compelled to.

The Way of Life, the strait gate, is, however, worth much more than whatever trouble or effort it may call for. On this road the rewards are not temporary but permanent; every mile gained is gained for all eternity. Indeed, the changing of one's consciousness is in truth the only thing that is really worth doing at all. A comparison from everyday life will help to illustrate this point: Suppose a man successfully removes a stain from his coat; that action will benefit him for as long as the garment is in use, say a few months. Suppose, on the other hand, he develops a bodily function, say his breathing capacity, by suitable physical exercises; the improvement gained here will be with him for the remainder of his physical life, perhaps fifty or sixty years, and is, for that reason alone, a far more important thing to have done, even apart from the much more far-reaching effect upon his life of the operation itself. Now, if he makes a *qualitative* change in his conscious-ness, which is what happens under prayer or treatment, then not only is the effect of that change felt in every phase and department of his life, but it is with him through all eternity, for he never can lose it. *Thieves cannot break in and steal.*

As soon as you obtain spiritual consciousness you will find that all things indeed work together for good to those who love Good, or God. You will experience perfect health, abundant prosperity, and complete and utter happiness. Your health will be so good that mere living will be in itself an inexpressible joy. The body, no longer the burden to be dragged about that so many people find it, will be as though it were shod with winged shoes. Your prosperity will be such that you need not take the question of finance into consideration at all. You will always have all the supply that you need to carry out any of your plans. The world will turn out to be full of charming people only too anxious to help you in every way. Others will come into your life only for good. You will find yourself occupied with the most delightful and interesting activities of the most widely useful kind. All your energy and all your faculties will find full scope for their expression and, in short, you will develop the "completely integrated and fully expressed personality" of which modern psychology dreams.

Those who have not glimpsed the secret of the Christ Message may look upon all this as nothing but a beautiful vision, "too good to be true," but it is just the essence of the Christ Message that nothing is too good to be true, because the Love and the Power of God are true. It is just this very belief that complete harmony is too good to be true that really prevents our getting it. We, as mental beings, make the laws under which we live; and we have to live under the laws that we make.

A tragic mistake that is often made by orthodox religious people is to assume that the Will of God for them is bound to be something very dull and uninviting, if not positively unpleasant. Consciously or not they look upon God as a hard taskmaster, or a severe Puritanical parent. Too often their prayers virtually amount to something like this: "Please, God, give me such and such a boon, which I sorely need— but I don't suppose you will, because you won't think it is good for me." Needless to say, a prayer of this sort is answered as all prayers are answered, according to the faith of the subject; that is to say, the boon is not granted. The truth is that the Will of God for us always means greater freedom, greater self-expression, wider and newer and brighter experience; better health, greater prosperity, wider opportunity of service to others—life more abundant.

If you are ill or in poverty, or obliged to do work that you dislike; if you are lonely, or if you have to mix with people who displease you; you may be certain that you are not expressing the Will of God, and as long as you are not expressing His Will, it is natural for you to experience inharmony; and it is equally true that when you do express His Will, harmony will come.

Beware of false prophets, which come to you in sheep's clothing, but inwardly they are ravening wolves.

Ye shall know them by their fruits. Do men gather grapes of thorns, or figs of thistles?

Even so every good tree bringeth forth good fruit; but a corrupt tree bringeth forth evil fruit.

A good tree cannot bring forth evil fruit, neither can a corrupt tree bring forth good fruit.

Every tree that bringeth not forth good fruit is hewn down, and cast into the fire.

Wherefore by their fruits ye shall know them.

—MATTHEW VII

Is there any infallible way in which man can find out the real Truth about God, and about life, and about himself? Is there any way in which he can tell for himself which is the true religion, and which is not? which of the churches are genuine and which are false? which books or teachers teach the Truth, and which teach error? How many honest seekers for Truth, confused and worried by the babel of conflicting theologies and brawling sects, have yearned with their whole hearts for some simple test whereby the honest seeker could discover for himself what the Truth really is?

Is there a single sincere Christian who would not eagerly strive to follow the wishes of Jesus Christ if only he could find out what they are? He is told by all sorts of people and by all sorts of churches that they alone represent the true teaching, and that he will disregard their doctrines and their discipline at his peril; and yet they all disagree among themselves upon vital points both of theory and practice; and each of them individually is full of inconsistencies.

If man really were left without a simple practical test of religious truth, he would assuredly be in a sad plight; but happily this is not the case. Jesus, the most profound, and at the same time the most simple and practical teacher the world has ever known, has provided for this need, and has given us an utterly simple and universally applicable test for Truth. It is a test that any man or woman of any kind, anywhere, can easily apply for himself. It is as simple and direct as the acid test for gold. It is the simple question—*Does it work?*

This test is so staggeringly simple that most clever people have passed it over as not worth considering, forgetting that all the great elemental things of life are simple. Yet, just this is the fundamental test for Truth—does it work?—because Truth always works. The Truth always heals. A true story always turns out to be consistent when thoroughly sifted, while the most plausible lie will break down somewhere if sufficiently investigated. Truth heals the body, purifies the soul, reforms the sinner, solves difficulties, pacifies strife. From this it follows that, according to Jesus, teaching that is true will automatically prove itself by practical demonstration. "They shall cast out devils, speak in new tongues, take up serpents, drink any deadly thing with impunity, and they shall lay hands upon the sick, and they shall recover." False teaching, on the contrary, no matter how attractively it may be presented, no matter what social or academic prestige may be attached to it, will fail to do all or any of these things; and, failing to measure up to the test, must be condemned. Its sponsors are false Prophets clad in the sheep's clothing of true religion; but, although they are usually perfectly sincere in their claims and pretensions, still they come between the seeker and the saving Truth, and are therefore, despite their good intentions, spiritual wolves. *By their fruits ye shall know them.*

Now that we understand clearly that a successful demonstration is the proof, and the only proof, of true understanding, we have no further excuse for straying from the Path. Our progress on the Path may, for one reason or another, be comparatively slow, but at least we shall be able to keep on the Path. We shall always know when we have left the Path, because demonstrations will cease. Most people find it especially difficult to demonstrate in certain directions, while having little difficulty in others. This is to be expected, and only means that more work needs to be done in some directions than in others. If, however, you are getting no real demonstrations in any direction, it means that you have left the Path and are no longer praying rightly; and you must immediately get back, by claiming that Divine Intelligence is inspiring you, and that you are expressing Truth. If you do this, you will come to no harm, even if the unproductive period seems to last rather a long time; and you will learn a good deal. But if, on the other hand, you behave like the Pharisees and, instead of frankly admitting your mistake, proceed to indulge in self-righteousness and spiritual pride, then indeed you are in for a bad time. If, like some misguided people, you say something like this: "I do not demonstrate, but I do not wish to do so, because I am too spiritual; I am above demonstration; I am too advanced for that kind of thing," or perhaps, "I demonstrate in ways that you cannot see"; then you are not merely talking nonsense, but you are doing something very like blaspheming Divine Wisdom itself—and what is this but the sin against the Holy Ghost?

One does not seek demonstrations as an end in themselves, but one seeks to know Truth as an end in itself; and since the Law is that as one acquires true understanding the outer picture improves automatically, that change in the outer picture becomes the visible evidence of the change in the inner—"an outward and visible sign of an inward and spiritual grace"—and thus we come to know unerringly where we stand. The outer picture is like the gauge that tells what is happening inside a boiler.

The real reason for desiring demonstrations is that they are the proof of understanding. *There is no such thing as undemonstrated understanding.* As within, so without; as without, so within. If you wish to know how you really stand spiritually, look about you at your environment, beginning with the body. There can be nothing in the soul that is not demonstrated sooner or later in the outer, and there can be nothing in the outer which does not find some correspondence in the inner.

Whether it be the testing of your own soul, or the test of a teacher, or the test of a book or a church, that test is always simple, direct, and infallible. Does it work? What are the fruits? *By their fruits ye shall know them.*

> *Not every one that saith unto me, Lord, Lord, shall enter into the kingdom of heaven; but he that doeth the will of my Father which is in heaven.*
>
> *Many will say to me in that day, Lord, Lord, have we not prophesied in thy name? and in thy name have cast out devils? and in thy name done many wonderful works?*
>
> *And then will I profess unto them, I never knew you: depart from me, ye that work iniquity.*
>
> —MATTHEW VII

Mankind is slow to realize that there is simply no way of salvation except by changing one's consciousness, which means trying to do the Will of God consistently in every department of life. We are all willing to do His Will sometimes and in some things, but until there is a complete alignment both in the great and in the small things—a complete dedication of one's whole self in fact—there cannot be a complete demonstration. As long as we are allowing any secondary thing to come between us and the Primary thing, there is no full salvation. "There is no home for the soul in which there dwells the shadow of an untruth," said George Meredith.

This danger is an extraordinarily subtle one. No sooner have we met and mastered it in one direction than it seems to attack us in another. It calls for nothing less than unceasing watchfulness, and an almost heroic courage. Never is it more true than in the life of the soul, that the price of liberty is eternal vigilance. We must not allow any consideration whatever, any institution, or organization, or any book, or any man or woman, to come between us and our direct seeking for God. If our reliance is upon anything but our own understanding of Truth, our work will cease to be fruitful. If we rely unduly upon anyone else, upon a particular teacher or healer, for instance, he will be certain to fail us, probably through no fault of his own. He will be out of reach when we most need him, or for some other reason will be unavailable in our hour of need. The same principle applies when people allow themselves to become the slaves of special conditions. A certain woman said: "I can treat myself only when I am in the reading room of our local center; the atmosphere there is so beautiful." The time came, and not very long afterwards, when her husband was transferred by the government to a mid-African station where she had to meet a crisis thousands of miles from a reading room, and more than a hundred miles from any other white woman. Then she was driven back on her real knowledge of Truth, and, of course, made a great advance in understanding.

It is your duty to get all the help that you can from books and teachers, and so forth; but unless your real reliance is upon your own understanding, you are only crying "Lord, Lord" with your lips, and pretending to prophesy in His name while essentially "knowing Him not"; which, for practical purposes, will be as though He knew you not. There is no entering the Kingdom of Heaven in this way. For the thousandth time let it be said, you have to earn your salvation by genuine, consistent hard work upon your own consciousness in realizing God.

Many people hesitate to free themselves from an orthodox church which they have really outgrown, because of the practical or merely sentimental inconvenience of breaking a family tradition; but "He that loveth father or mother more than me is not worthy of me." Again, many people seem to find it possible to summon up enough energy and courage to break from the orthodox church, only to settle down once more, almost as inertly, into one of the more liberal churches, or into some spiritual center or organization, where they seem to go to sleep again, under the impression that they have now at last discovered the Truth, and need take no further trouble. As if this were not exactly the same old mistake made by the pioneers and founders of all the orthodox churches themselves; all of which originally started as reforming heresies. What do you gain by breaking free from one organization if you are only going to surrender your newfound freedom to another one?

In other cases people have developed a personal devotion to some independent teacher which has caused them entirely to yield their own judgment to his. Others again have some favorite textbook which, in fact if not in name, they regard as infallible.

Now the only infallible thing known to man is the simple test for Truth that Jesus gave us—*By their fruits ye shall know them.*

You should gladly take advantage of helpful teaching wherever you may get it; go to churches or meetings that help you; listen to speakers, and read books that inspire you to find yourself; but do not surrender to anybody your own spiritual judgment. Thank those who have helped you, and acknowledge the good received; but always be ready to pass on to the next step. Remember that the Truth of Being concerns Itself with the infinite, the impersonal Principle of Life; and does not lend Itself to the exploitation of particular personalities or organizations. You do not owe an atom of loyalty to anyone or anything in the universe except your own Indwelling Christ, your own spiritual integrity. If merely enrolling oneself in the membership of some organized body were a guarantee of spiritual understanding, our salvation would be a much simpler matter than it is. Unfortunately the problem is much more involved. Centers, churches, schools, all fill a useful purpose in providing the physical framework for the distribution of right knowledge, through lectures, books, and so forth; but the actual work must be done in the individual consciousness. To claim more than this for outer things is to reestablish superstition. If, when the testing time comes, we attempt to lean upon a church membership, or upon our devotion to a teacher's personality, or upon a mere letter-perfect acquaintance with any textbook, the Voice of Truth will proclaim that it never knew us; and we shall have to go without our demonstration.

Because human life and human character are so many-sided, the Bible approaches every problem from several different angles. This section of the Sermon teaches another very important lesson too; namely, that the only true way of bringing about anything is by the Practice of the Presence of

God. This is the only way in which permanent results can be obtained. Temporary alterations in conditions may be achieved by will power, but they are only temporary, and sooner or later anything that seems to have been accomplished in this way will disappear again, leaving everything worse than it was before. A great fortune, for instance, may be built up by will power alone, but money thus acquired sooner or later takes wings unto itself and flies away again, leaving its deluded victim poorer than ever. Such a person knows not the Truth of Being, and therefore it knows him not, and cannot help him. Dramatically stated, in the Oriental way, this becomes: *I never knew you: depart from me, ye that work iniquity.*

When a person has made such a mistake as this the thing for him to do is promptly to discontinue trying to work without God, whereupon his mistake will be forgiven, as all mistakes are, as soon as we repent of them. Then he should immediately begin to work for supply on the Spiritual Basis, claiming God as his Source and realizing the bounty of God as his. Thus he will build up a true prosperity consciousness, and when this is done he never can be impoverished.

Therefore whosoever heareth these sayings of mine, and doeth them, I will liken him unto a wise man, which built his home upon a rock:

And the rain descended, and the floods came, and the winds blew, and beat upon that house; and it fell not: for it was founded upon a rock.

And every one that heareth these sayings of mine, and doeth them not, shall be likened unto a foolish man, which built his house upon the sand:

And the rain descended, and the floods came, and the winds blew, and beat upon that house; and it fell: and great was the fall of it.

—MATTHEW VII

The Sermon concludes with one of those illustrations that for simplicity, directness, and graphic power are unmatched outside the teaching of Jesus. No one who has read this parable of the two houses can ever forget it. It warns us once again of the vanity of precept without practice; of the deadly peril of those who know the Truth, or at least know about it, without honestly trying as well as they can to put it into practice. One could almost say, better never to have heard of the Truth at all, than to know of it and not try to live it.

One of the very oldest and most important symbols for the human soul is that of a building, sometimes a dwelling house, and sometimes a Temple, which man is occupied in building. Man the Builder is as familiar a character in the Occult Tradition as man the Shepherd, or man the Fisherman, or man the King, as we found him in an earlier section. The first thing that has to be done by the builder of a house is to select a sound foundation, for, without that, it matters not how skillfully and conscientiously the building is put up, it will collapse under the first serious storm that comes along. Jesus, we remember, was brought up in the home and workshop of a carpenter, who, in that time and place, would be a builder too, as he still often is in remote country places among ourselves; and this illustration is one that would immediately occur to him. On the shifting sands of the desert it is impossible to build anything at all, and so there people have to dwell in tents. When the Oriental intends to put up a permanent structure he looks about for a rock, and builds upon that. Now the Rock is one of the Bible terms for the Christ, and the implication is very obvious. The Christ Truth is the one and only foundation upon which we can build the Temple of the regenerated soul with safety. It is the one thing in existence that is absolutely true, never varying, never shifting—the same yesterday, today, and forever. Resting upon this foundation we shall stand secure when the winds, and rains, and floods of error, of fear, and doubt, and self-reproach, beat upon us, beat they ever so hard; for we are founded upon the Rock. But as long as we are depending upon anything less than the Rock— upon will power, upon so-called material security, upon the goodwill of others, or upon our own personal resources—

upon anything but God in fact, we are building upon sand, and great will be our fall.

> *And it came to pass, when Jesus had ended these sayings, the people were astonished at his doctrine:*
>
> *For he taught them as one having authority, and not as the scribes.*
>
> —MATTHEW VII

In this concluding paragraph we are told quite simply that the people were astonished at his doctrine. It is always so. The Jesus Christ message is utterly revolutionary. It reverses all the standards and all the methods, not only of the "world," but of all conventional or orthodox religion itself, for it turns our gaze from the outside to the inside, and from man and his works to God.

He taught as one having authority, and not as the scribes. The greatest glory of the Spiritual Basis is that you begin to *know.* When you have obtained the smallest true demonstration by means of scientific prayer, you have experienced something that never leaves you. You have the witness of Truth within yourself. You are no longer dependent upon the word of somebody else; you know for yourself; and this is the only authority worth having. Jesus had this authority and he proved it by doing the works. In the next chapter of Matthew we learn that immediately after the last discourse in this Sermon on the Mount, on his way back to the town in fact, he instantaneously healed a leper. This was proving that his doctrines were not mere theorizing; and proving it with a vengeance.

Jesus contacted God direct, and there when he spoke, he spoke the Word of Power.

THE LORD'S PRAYER

PRAYER

AN INTERPRETATION

He prayeth well who loveth well

Both man and bird and beast;

He prayeth best who loveth best

All things both great and small:

For the dear God who loveth us,

He made and loveth all.

—COLERIDGE

Our Father, which art in heaven, Hallowed be thy name. Thy kingdom come. Thy will be done, in earth as it is in heaven. Give us this day our daily bread. And forgive us our trespasses, as we forgive them that trespass against us. And lead us not into temptation; but deliver us from evil: For thine is the kingdom, the power, and the glory, for ever and ever.

Amen.

THE LORD'S PRAYER

The Lord's Prayer is the most important of all the Christian documents. It was carefully constructed by Jesus with certain very clear ends in view. That is why, of all his teachings, it is by far the best known, and the most often quoted. It is, indeed, the one common denominator of all the Christian churches. Every one of them, without exception, uses the Lord's Prayer; it is perhaps the only ground upon which they all meet. Every Christian child is taught the Lord's Prayer, and any Christian who prays at all says it almost every day. Its actual use probably exceeds that of all other prayers put together. Undoubtedly everyone who is seeking to follow along the Way that Jesus led, should make a point of using the Lord's Prayer, and using it intelligently, every day.

In order to do this, we should understand that the Prayer is a carefully constructed organic whole. Many people rattle through it like parrots, forgetful of the warning that Jesus gave us against vain repetitions, and, of course, no one derives any profit from that sort of thing.

The Great Prayer is a compact formula for the development of the soul. It is designed with the utmost care for the specific purpose; so that those who use it regularly, with understanding, will experience a real change of soul. The only progress is this change, which is what the Bible calls being born again. It is the change of soul that matters. The mere acquisition of fresh knowledge received intellectually makes no change in the soul. The Lord's Prayer is especially designed to bring this change about, and when it is regularly used it invariably does so.

The more one analyzes the Lord's Prayer, the more wonderful is its construction seen to be. It meets everyone's need just at his own level. It not only provides a rapid spiritual development for those who are sufficiently advanced to be ready, but in its superficial meaning it supplies the more simpleminded and even the more materially-minded people with just what they need at the moment, if they use the Prayer sincerely.

This greatest of all prayers was designed with still another purpose in view, quite as important as either of the others. Jesus foresaw that, as the centuries went by, his simple, primitive teaching would gradually become overlain by all sorts of external things which really have nothing whatever to do with it. He foresaw that men who had never known him, relying, quite sincerely, no doubt, upon their own limited intellects, would build up theologies and doctrinal systems, obscuring the direct simplicity of the spiritual message, and actually erecting a wall between God and man. He designed his Prayer in such a way that it would pass safely through those ages without being tampered with. He arranged it with consummate skill, so that it could not be twisted or distorted, or adapted to any man-made system; so that, in fact, it would carry the whole Christ Message within it, and yet not have anything on the surface to attract the attention of the restless, managing type of person. So it has turned out that, through all the changes and chances of Christian history, this Prayer has come through to us uncorrupted and unspoiled.

The first thing that we notice is that the Prayer naturally falls into seven clauses. This is very characteristic of the Oriental tradition. Seven symbolizes individual completeness, the perfection of the individual soul, just as the number twelve in the same convention stands for corporate completeness. In practical use, we often find an eighth clause added—"Thine is the kingdom, the power, and the glory"—but this, though in itself an excellent affirmation, is not really a part of the Prayer. The seven clauses are put together with the utmost care, in perfect order and sequence, and they contain everything that is necessary for the nourishment of the soul. Let us consider the first clause.

OUR FATHER

This simple statement in itself constitutes a definite and complete system of theology. It fixes clearly and distinctly the nature and character of God. It sums up the Truth of Being. It tells all that man needs to know about God, and about himself, and about his neighbor. Anything that is added to this can only be by way of commentary, and is more likely than not to complicate and obscure the true meaning of the text. Oliver Wendell Holmes said: "My religion is summed up in the first two words of the Lord's Prayer," and most of us will find ourselves in full agreement with him.

Notice the simple, clear-cut, definite statement—"Our Father." In this clause Jesus lays down once and for all that the relationship between God and man is that of father and child. This cuts out any possibility that the Deity could be the relentless and cruel tyrant that is often pictured by theology. Jesus says definitely that the relationship is that of parent and child; not an Oriental despot dealing with grovelling slaves, but parent and child. Now we all know perfectly well that men and women, however short they may fall in other respects, nearly always do the best they can for their children. Unfortunately, cruel and wicked parents are to be found, but they are so exceptional as to make a paragraph for the newspapers. The vast majority of men and women are at their best in dealing with their children. Speaking of the same truth elsewhere, Jesus said: "If you, who are so full of evil, nevertheless do your best for your children, how much more will God, who is altogether good, do for you"; and so he begins his Prayer by establishing the character of God as that of the perfect Father dealing with His children.

Note that this clause which fixes the nature of God, at the same time fixes the nature of man, because if man is the offspring of God, he must partake of the nature of God, since the nature of the offspring is invariably similar to that of the parent. It is a cosmic law that like begets like. It is not possible that a rosebush should produce lilies, or that a cow should give birth to a colt. The offspring is and must be of the same nature as the parent; and so, since God is Divine Spirit, man must essentially be Divine Spirit too, whatever appearances may say to the contrary.

Let us pause here for a moment and try to realize what a tremendous step forward we have taken in appreciating the teaching of Jesus on this point. Do you not see that at a single blow it swept away ninety-nine per cent of all the old theology, with its avenging God, its chosen and favored individuals, its eternal hell fire, and all the other horrible paraphernalia of man's diseased and terrified imagination. God exists—and the Eternal, All-Powerful, All-Present God is the loving Father of mankind.

If you would meditate upon this fact, until you had some degree of understanding of what it really means, most of your difficulties and physical ailments would disappear, for they are rooted and grounded in fear. The underlying cause of *all* trouble is fear. If only you could realize to some extent that Omnipotent Wisdom is your living, loving Father, most of your fears would go. If you could realize it completely, every negative thing in your life would vanish away, and you would demonstrate perfection in every phase. Now you see the object that Jesus had in mind when he placed this clause first.

Next we see that the Prayer says, not "My Father," but "Our Father," and this indicates, beyond the possibility of mistake, the truth of the brotherhood of man. It forces upon our attention at the very beginning the fact that all men are indeed brethren, the children of one Father; and that "there is neither Jew nor Greek, there is neither bond nor free, there is neither chosen nor unchosen," because all men are brethren. Here Jesus in making his second point, ends all the tiresome nonsense about a "chosen race," about the spiritual superiority of any one group of human beings over any other group. He cuts away the illusion that the members of any nation, or race, or territory, or group, or class, or color, are, in the sight of God, superior to any other group. A belief in the superiority of one's own particular group, or "herd," as the psychologists call it, is an illusion to which mankind is very prone, but in the teaching of Jesus it has no place. He teaches that the thing that places a man is the spiritual condition of his own individual soul, and that as long as he is upon the spiritual path it makes no difference whatever to what group he belongs or does not belong.

The final point is the implied command that we are to pray not only for ourselves but for all mankind. Every student of Truth should hold the thought of the Truth of Being for the whole human race for at least a moment each day, since none of us lives to himself nor dies to himself; for indeed we are all truly—and in a much more literal sense than people are aware—limbs of one Body.

Now we begin to see how very much more than appears on the surface is contained in those simple words "Our Father." Simple—one might almost say innocent—as they look, Jesus has concealed within them a spiritual explosive that will ultimately destroy every man-made system that holds the human race in bondage.

WHICH ART
IN HEAVEN

Having clearly established the Fatherhood of God and the brotherhood of man, Jesus next goes on to enlarge upon the nature of God, and to describe the fundamental facts of existence. Having shown that God and man are parent and child, he goes on to delineate the function of each in the grand scheme of things. He explains that it is the nature of God to be in heaven, and of man to be on earth, because God is Cause, and man is manifestation. Cause cannot be expression, and expression cannot be cause, and we must be careful not to confuse the two things. Here heaven stands for God or Cause, because in religious phraseology heaven is the term for the Presence of God. In metaphysics it is called the Absolute, because it is the realm of Pure Unconditioned Being, of archetypal ideas. The word "earth" means manifestation, and man's function is to manifest or express God, or Cause. In other words, God is the Infinite and Perfect Cause of all things; but Cause has to be expressed, and God expresses Himself by means of man. Man's destiny is to express God in all sorts of glorious and wonderful ways. Some of this expression we see as his surroundings; first his physical body, which is really only the most intimate part of his embodiment; then his home; his work; his recreation; in short, his whole expression. To express means to press outwards, or bring into sight that which already exists implicitly. Every feature of your life is really a manifestation or expression of something in your soul.

Some of these points may seem at first to be a little abstract; but since it is misunderstandings about the relationship of God and man that lead to all our difficulties, it is worth any amount of trouble to correctly understand that relationship. Trying to have manifestation without Cause is atheism and materialism, and we know where they lead. Trying to have Cause without manifestation leads man to suppose himself to be a personal God, and this commonly ends in megalomania and a kind of paralysis of expression.

The important thing to realize is that God is in heaven and man on earth, and that each has his own role in the scheme of things. Although they are One, they are not one-and-the-same. Jesus establishes this point carefully when he says, "Our Father which art in heaven."

HALLOWED BE
THY NAME

In the Bible, as elsewhere, the "name" of anything means the essential nature or character of that thing, and so, when we are told what the name of God is, we are told what His nature is, and His name or nature, Jesus says, is "hallowed." Now what does the word "hallowed" mean? Well, if you trace the derivation back into Old English, you will discover a most extraordinarily interesting and significant fact. The word "hallowed" has the same meaning as "holy," "whole," "wholesome," and "heal," or "healed"; so we see that the nature of God is not merely worthy of our veneration, but is complete and perfect—altogether good. Some very remarkable consequences follow from this. We have agreed that an effect must be similar in its nature to its cause, and so, because the nature of God is hallowed, everything that follows from that Cause must be hallowed or perfect too. Just as a rosebush cannot produce lilies, so God cannot cause or send anything but perfect good. As the Bible says, "The same fountain cannot send forth both sweet and bitter water." From this it follows that God cannot, as people sometimes think, send sickness or trouble, or accidents—much less death—for these things are unlike His nature. "Hallowed be thy name" means "Thy nature is altogether good, and Thou art the author only of perfect good." *Of purer eyes than to behold evil, and canst not look on iniquity.*

If you think that God has sent any of your difficulties to you, for no matter how good a reason, you are giving power to your troubles, and this makes it very difficult to get rid of them.

THY KINGDOM
COME THY WILL
BE DONE IN EARTH
AS IT IS IN HEAVEN

Man being *manifestation* or expression of God has a limitless destiny before him. His work is to express, in concrete, definite form, the abstract ideas with which God furnishes him, and in order to do this, he must have creative power. If he did not have creative power, he would be merely a machine through which God worked—an automation. But man is not an automation; he is an individualized consciousness. God individualizes Himself in an infinite number of distinct focal points of consciousness, each one quite different; and therefore each one is a distinct way of knowing the universe, each a distinct experience. Notice carefully that the word "individual" means *undivided*. The consciousness of each one is distinct from God and from all others, and yet none are separated. How can this be? How can two things be one, and yet not one and the same? The answer is that in matter, which is finite, they cannot; but in Spirit, which is infinite, they can. With our present limited, three-dimensional consciousness, we cannot see this; but intuitively we can understand it through prayer. If God did not individualize Himself, there would be only one experience; as it is, there are as many universes as there are individuals to form them through thinking.

"Thy kingdom come" means that it is our duty to be ever occupied in helping to establish the Kingdom of God on earth. That is to say, our work is to bring more and more of God's ideas into concrete manifestation upon this plane. That is what we are here for. The old saying, "God has a plan for every man, and he has one for you," is quite correct. God has glorious and wonderful plans for every one of us; He has planned a splendid career, full of interest, life, and joy, for each, and if our lives are dull, or restricted, or squalid, that is not His fault, but ours.

If only you will find out the thing God intends you to do, and will do it, you will find that all doors will open to you; all obstacles in your path will melt away; you will be acclaimed a brilliant success; you will be most liberally rewarded from the monetary point of view; and you will be gloriously happy.

There is a true place in life for each one of us, upon the attainment of which we shall be completely happy, and perfectly secure. On the other hand, until we do find our true place we never shall be either happy or secure, no matter what other things we may have. Our true place is the one place where we can bring the Kingdom of God into manifestation, and truly say, "Thy kingdom cometh."

We have seen that man too often chooses to use his free will in a negative way. He allows himself to think wrongly, selfishly, and this wrong thinking brings upon him all his troubles. Instead of understanding that it is his essential nature to express God, to be ever about his Father's business, he tries to set up upon his own account. All our troubles arise from just this folly. We abuse our free will, trying to work apart from God; and the very natural result is all the sickness, poverty, sin, trouble, and death that we find on the physical plane. We must never for a moment try to live for ourselves, or make plans or arrangements without reference to God, or suppose that we can be either happy or successful if we are seeking any other end than to do His Will. Whatever our desire may be, whether it be something concerning our daily work, or our duty at home, our relations with our fellowman, or private plans for the employment of our own time, if we seek to serve self instead of God, we are ordering trouble, disappointment, and unhappiness, notwithstanding what the evidence to the contrary may seem to be. Whereas, if we choose what, through prayer, we know to be His Will, then we are insuring for ourselves ultimate success, freedom, and joy, however much self-sacrifice and self-discipline it may involve at the moment.

Our business is to bring our whole nature as fast as we can into conformity with the Will of God, by constant prayer and unceasing, though unanxious, watching. "Our wills are ours to make them Thine."

"In His Will is our peace," said Dante, and the *Divine Comedy* is really a study in fundamental states of consciousness, the *Inferno* representing the state of the soul that is endeavoring to live without God, the *Paradiso* representing the state of the soul that has achieved its conscious unity with the Divine Will, and the *Purgatorio* the condition of the soul that is struggling to pass from the one state to the other. It was this sublime conflict of the soul which wrung from the heart of the great Augustine the cry "Thou hast made us for Thyself, and our hearts are restless until they repose in Thee."

GIVE US THIS DAY
OUR DAILY BREAD

Because we are the children of a loving Father, we are entitled to expect that God will provide us fully with everything we need. Children naturally and spontaneously look to their human parents to supply all their wants, and in the same way we should look to God to supply ours. If we do so, in faith and understanding, we shall never look in vain.

It is the Will of God that we should all lead healthy, happy lives, full of joyous experience; that we should develop freely and steadily, day by day and week by week, as our pathways unfold more and more unto the perfect day. To this end we require such things as food, clothing, shelter, means of travel, books, and so on; above all, we require *freedom;* and in the Prayer all these things are included under the heading of bread. Bread, that is to say, means not merely food in general, but all things that man requires for a healthy, happy, free, and harmonious life. But in order to obtain these things, we have to claim them, not necessarily in detail, but *we have to claim them,* and, we have to recognize God and God alone as the Source and fountainhead of all our good. Lack of any kind is always traceable to the fact that we have been seeking our supply from some secondary source, instead of from God, Himself, the Author and Giver of life.

People think of their supply as coming from certain investments, or from a business, or from an employer, perhaps; whereas these are merely the channels through which it comes, God being the Source. The number of possible channels is infinite, the Source is One. The particular channel through which you are getting your supply is quite likely to change, because change is the Cosmic Law for manifestation. Stagnation is really death; but as long as you realize that the *Source* of your supply is the one unchangeable Spirit, all is well. The fading out of one channel will be but the signal for the opening of another. If, on the other hand, like most people, you regard the particular channel as being the source, then when that channel fails, as it is very likely to do, you are left stranded, because you *believe* that the source has dried up—and for practical purposes, on the physical plane, things are as we believe them to be.

A man, for instance, thinks of his employment as the

source of his income, and for some reason he loses it. His employer goes out of business, or cuts down the staff, or they have a falling out. Now, because he believes that his position is the source of his income, the loss of the position naturally means the loss of the income, and so he has to start looking about for another job, and perhaps has to look a long time, meanwhile finding himself without apparent supply. If such a man had realized, through regular daily Treatment, that God was his supply, and his job only the particular channel through which it came, then upon the closing of that channel, he would have found another, and probably a better one, opening immediately. If his belief had been in God as his supply, then since God cannot change or fail, or fade out, his supply would have come from *somewhere,* and would have formed its own channel in whatever was the easiest way.

In precisely the same way the proprietor of a business may find himself obliged to close down for some cause outside of his control; or one whose income is dependent upon stocks or bonds may suddenly find that source dried up, owing to unexpected happenings on the stock market, or to some catastrophe to a factory or a mine. If he regards the business or the investment as his *source* of supply, he will believe his source to have collapsed, and will in consequence be left stranded; whereas, if his reliance is upon God, he will be comparatively indifferent to the channel and so that channel will be easily supplanted by a new one. In short, we have to train ourselves to look to God, Cause, for all that we need, and then the channel, which is entirely a secondary matter, will take care of itself.

In its inner and most important meaning, our daily bread signifies the realization of the Presence of God—an actual sense that God exists not merely in a nominal way, but as *the* great reality; the sense that He is present with us; and the feeling that because He is God, all-good, all-powerful, all-wise, and all-loving, we have nothing to fear; that we can rely upon Him to take every care of us; that He will supply all that we need to have; teach us all that we need to know; and guide our steps so that we shall not make mistakes. This is Emanuel, or God with us; and remember that it absolutely means some degree of actual *realization,* that is to say, some experience in consciousness, and not just a theoretical recognition of the fact; not simply talking about God, however beautifully one may talk, or *thinking about* Him; but some degree of actual experience. We must begin by thinking about God, but this should lead to the realization which is the *daily bread* or manna. That is the gist of the whole matter. Realization, which is experience, is the thing that counts. It is realization which marks the progress of the soul. It is realization which guarantees the demonstration. It is realization, as distinct from mere theorizing and fine words, which is the *substance of things hoped for, the evidence of things not seen.* This is the Bread of Life, the hidden manna, and when one has that, he has all things in deed and in truth. Jesus several times refers to this experience as bread because it is the nourishment of the soul, just a physical food is the nourishment of the physical body. Supplied with this food, the soul grows and waxes strong, gradually developing to adult stature. Without it, she, being deprived of her essential nourishment, is naturally stunted and crippled.

The common mistake, of course, is to suppose that a formal recognition of God is sufficient, or that talking about Divine things, perhaps talking very poetically, is the same as possessing them; but this is exactly on a par with supposing that looking at a tray of food, or discussing the chemical composition of sundry foodstuffs, is the same thing as actually eating a meal. It is this mistake which is responsible for the fact that people sometimes pray for a thing for years without any tangible result. If prayer is a force at all, it cannot be possible to pray without something happening.

A realization cannot be obtained to order; it must come spontaneously as the result of regular daily prayer. To seek realization by will power is the surest way to miss it. Pray regularly and quietly—remember that in all mental work, *effort* or strain defeats itself—then presently, perhaps when you least expect it, like a thief in the night, the realization will come. Meanwhile it is well to know that all sorts of practical difficulties can be overcome by sincere prayer, without any realization at all. Good workers have said that they have had some of their best demonstrations without any realization worth speaking about; but while it is, of course, a wonderful boon to surmount such particular difficulties, we do not achieve the sense of security and well-being to which we are entitled until we have experienced realization.

Another reason why the food or bread symbol for the experience of the Presence of God is such a telling one is that the act of eating food is essentially a thing that must be done for oneself. No one can assimilate food for another. One may hire servants to do all sorts of other things for him; but there is one thing that one must positively do for himself, and that is to eat his own food. In the same way, the realization of the Presence of God is a thing that no one else can have for us. We can and should help one another in the overcoming of specific difficulties—"Bear ye one another's burdens"—but the realization (or making real) of the Presence of God, the "substance" and "evidence," can, in the nature of things, be had only at firsthand.

In speaking of the "bread of life, Emanuel," Jesus calls it our *daily* bread. The reason for this is very fundamental—our contact with God must be a living one. It is our *momentary* attitude to God which governs our being. "Behold *now* is the accepted time; behold *now* is the day of salvation." The most futile thing in the world is to seek to live upon a past realization. The thing that means spiritual life to you is your realization of God *here and now*.

Today's realization, no matter how feeble and poor it may seem, has a million times more power to help you than the most vivid realization of yesterday. Be thankful for yesterday's experience, knowing that it is with you forever in the change of consciousness which it brought about, but do not lean upon it for a single moment for the need of today. Divine Spirit *is,* and changes not with the ebb and flow of human apprehension. The manna in the desert is the Old Testament prototype of this. The people wandering in the wilderness were told that they would be supplied with manna from heaven every day, each one always receiving abundant for his needs, but they were on no account to try to save it up for the morrow. They were on no account to endeavor to live upon yesterday's food, and when, notwithstanding the rule, some of them did try to do so, the result was pestilence or death.

So it is with us. When we seek to live upon yesterday's realization, we are actually seeking to live in the past, and to live in the past is death. The art of life is to live in the present moment, and to make that moment as perfect as we can by the realization that we are the instruments and expression of God Himself. The best way to prepare for tomorrow is to make today all that it should be.

FORGIVE US OUR TRESPASSES, AS WE FORGIVE THEM THAT TRESPASS AGAINST US

This clause is the turning point of the Prayer. It is the strategic key to the whole Treatment. Let us notice here that Jesus has so arranged this marvelous Prayer that it covers the entire ground of the unfoldment of our souls completely, and in the most concise and telling way. It omits nothing that is essential for our salvation, and yet, so compact is it that there is not a thought or a word too much. Every idea fits into its place with perfect harmony and in perfect sequence. Anything more would be redundance, anything less would be incompleteness, and at this point it takes up the critical factor of forgiveness.

Having told us what God is, what man is, how the universe works, how we are to do our own work—the salvation of humanity and of our own souls—he then explains what our true nourishment or supply is, and the way in which we can obtain it; and now he comes to the forgiveness of sins.

The forgiveness of sins is the central problem of life. Sin is a sense of separation from God, and is the major tragedy of human experience. It is, of course, rooted in selfishness. It is essentially an attempt to gain some supposed good to which we are not entitled in justice. It is a sense of isolated, self-regarding, personal existence, whereas the Truth of Being is that all is One. Our true selves are at one with God, undivided from Him, expressing His ideas, witnessing to His nature—the dynamic Thinking of that Mind. Because we are all one with the great Whole of which we are spiritually a part, it follows that we are one with all men. Just because in Him we live and move and have our being, we are, in the absolute sense, all essentially one.

Evil, sin, the fall of man, in fact, is essentially the attempt to negate this Truth in our thoughts. We try to live apart from God. We try to do without Him. We act as though we had life of our own, as separate minds; as though we could have plans and purposes and interests separate from His. All this, if it were true, would mean that existence is not one and harmonious, but a chaos of competition and strife. It would mean that we are quite separate from our fellow man and could injure him, rob him, or hurt him, or even destroy him, without any damage to ourselves, and, in fact, that the more we took from other people the more we should have for ourselves. It would mean that the more we considered our own interests, and the more indifferent we were to the welfare of others, the better off we should be. Of course it would then follow naturally that it would pay others to treat us in the same way, and that accordingly we might expect many of them to do so. Now if this were true, it would mean that the whole universe is only a jungle, and that sooner or later it must destroy itself by its own inherent weakness and anarchy. But, of course, it is not true, and therein lies the joy of life.

Undoubtedly, many people do act as though they believed it to be true, and a great many more, who would be dreadfully shocked if brought face-to-face with that proposition in cold blood, have, nevertheless, a vague feeling that such must be very much the way things are, even though they, themselves, are personally above consciously acting in accordance with such a notion. Now this is the real basis of sin, of resentment, of condemnation, of jealousy, of remorse, and all the evil brood that walk that path.

This belief in independent and separate existence is the arch sin, and now, before we can progress any further, we have to take the knife to this evil thing and cut it out once and for all. Jesus knew this, and with this definite end in view he inserted at this critical point a carefully prepared statement that would compass our end and his, without the shadow of a possibility of miscarrying. He inserted what is nothing less than a trip clause. He drafted a declaration which would force us, without any conceivable possibility of escape, evasion, mental reservation, or subterfuge of any kind, to execute the great sacrament of forgiveness in all its fullness and far-reaching power.

As we repeat the Great Prayer intelligently, considering and meaning what we say, we are suddenly, so to speak, caught up off our feet and grasped as though in a vise, so that we must face this problem—and there is no escape. We must positively and definitely extend forgiveness to everyone to whom it is possible that we can owe forgiveness, namely, to anyone who we think can have injured us in any way. Jesus leaves no room for any possible glossing of this fundamental thing. He has constructed his Prayer with more skill than any lawyer displayed in the casting of a deed. He has so contrived it that once our attention has been drawn to this matter, we are inevitably obliged either to forgive our enemies in sincerity and truth, or never again to repeat that prayer. It is safe to say that no one who reads this with understanding will ever again be able to use the Lord's Prayer unless and until he has forgiven. Should you now attempt to repeat it without forgiving, it can safely be predicted that you will not be able to finish it. This great central clause will stick in your throat.

Notice that Jesus does not say, "Forgive me my trespasses and I will try to forgive others," or "I will see if it can be done," or "I will forgive generally, with certain exceptions." He obliges us to declare that we have actually forgiven, and forgiven all, *and he makes our claim to our own forgiveness to depend upon that.* Who is there who has grace enough to say his prayers at all, who does not long for the forgiveness or cancellation of his own mistakes and faults. Who would be so insane as to endeavor to seek the Kingdom of God without desiring to be relieved of his own sense of guilt. No one, we may believe. And so we see that we are trapped in the inescapable position that we cannot demand our own release before we have released our brother.

The forgiveness of others is the vestibule of Heaven, and Jesus knew it, and has led us to the door. You must forgive everyone who has ever hurt you if you want to be forgiven yourself; that is the long and the short of it. You have to get rid of all resentment and condemnation of others, and, not least, of self-condemnation and remorse. You have to forgive others, and having discontinued your own mistakes, you have to accept the forgiveness of God for them too, or you cannot make any progress. You have to forgive yourself, but you cannot forgive yourself sincerely until you have forgiven others first. Having forgiven others, you must be prepared to forgive yourself too, for to refuse to forgive one-self is only spiritual pride. "And by that sin fell the angels." We cannot make this point too clear to ourselves; we have got to forgive. There are few people in the world who have not at some time or other been hurt, really hurt, by someone else; or been disappointed, or injured, or deceived, or mis-led. Such things sink into the memory where they usually cause inflamed and festering wounds, and there is only one remedy—they have to be plucked out and thrown away. And the one and only way to do that is by forgiveness.

Of course, nothing in all the world is easier than to forgive people who have not hurt us very much. Nothing is easier than to rise above the thought of a trifling loss. Anybody will be willing to do this, but what the Law of Being requires of us is that we forgive not only these trifles, but the very things that are so hard to forgive that at first it seems impos-sible to do it at all. The despairing heart cries, "It is too much to ask. That thing meant too much to me. It is impossible. I cannot forgive it." But the Lord's Prayer makes our own for-giveness from God, which means our escape from guilt and limitation, dependent upon just this very thing. There is no escape from this, and so forgiveness there must be, no mat-ter how deeply we may have been injured, or how terribly we have suffered. It must be done.

If your prayers are not being answered, search your con-sciousness and see if there is not someone whom you have yet to forgive. Find out if there is not some old thing about which you are very resentful. Search and see if you are not really holding a grudge (it may be camouflaged in some self-righteous way) against some individual, or some body of people, a nation, a race, a social class, some religious movement of which you disapprove perhaps, a political party, or whatnot. If you are doing so, then you have an act of forgiveness to perform, and when this is done, you will probably make your demonstration. If you cannot forgive at present, you will have to wait for your demonstration until you can, and you will have to postpone finishing your recital of the Lord's Prayer too, or involve yourself in the position that you do not desire the forgiveness of God.

Setting others free means setting yourself free, because resentment is really a form of attachment. It is a Cosmic Truth that it takes two to make a prisoner: the prisoner—and a gaoler. There is no such thing as being a prisoner on one's own account. Every prisoner must have a gaoler, and the gaoler is as much as prisoner as his charge. When you hold resentment against anyone, you are bound to that person by a cosmic link, a real, though mental chain. You are tied by a cosmic tie to the thing that you hate. The one person perhaps in the whole world whom you most dislike is the very one to whom you are attaching yourself by a hook that is stronger than steel. Is this what you wish? Is this the condition in which you desire to go on living? Remember, you belong to the thing with which you are linked in thought, and at some time or other, if that tie endures, the object of your resentment will be drawn again into your life, perhaps to work further havoc. Do you think that you can afford this? Of course, no one can afford such a thing; and so the way is clear. You must cut all such ties, by a clear and spiritual act of forgiveness. You must loose him and let him go. By forgiveness you set yourself free; you save your soul. And because the law of love works alike for one and all, you help to save his soul too, making it just so much easier for him to become what he ought to be.

But how, in the name of all that is wise and good, is the magic act of forgiveness to be accomplished, when we have been so deeply injured that, though we have long wished with all our hearts that we could forgive, we have nevertheless found it impossible; when we have tried and tried to forgive, but have found the task beyond us.

The technique of forgiveness is simple enough, and not very difficult to manage when you understand how. The only thing that is essential is *willingness* to forgive. Provided you desire to forgive the offender, the greater part of the work is already done. People have always made such a bogey of forgiveness because they have been under the erroneous impression that to forgive a person means that you have to compel yourself to like him. Happily this is by no means the case—we are not called upon to like anyone whom we do not find ourselves liking spontaneously, and, indeed, it is quite impossible to like people to order. You can no more *like* to order than you can hold the winds in your fist, and if you endeavor to coerce yourself into doing so, you will finish by disliking or hating the offender more than ever. People used to think that when someone had hurt them very much, it was their duty, as good Christians, to pump up, as it were, a feeling of liking for him; and since such a thing is utterly impossible, they suffered a great deal of distress, and ended, necessarily, with failure, and a resulting sense of sinfulness. We are not obliged to like anyone; but we are under a binding obligation to love everyone, love, or charity as the Bible calls it, meaning a vivid sense of impersonal good will. This has nothing directly to do with the feelings, though it is always *followed*, sooner or later, by a wonderful feeling of peace and happiness.

The method of forgiving is this: Get by yourself and become quiet. Repeat any prayer or treatment that appeals to you, or read a chapter of the Bible. Then quietly say, "I fully and freely forgive X (mentioning the name of the offender); I loose him and let him go. I completely forgive the whole business in question. As far as I am concerned, it is finished forever. I cast the burden of resentment upon the Christ within me. He is free now, and I am free too. I wish him well in every phase of his life. That incident is finished. The Christ Truth has set us both free. I thank God." Then get up and go about your business. On no account repeat this act of forgiveness, because you have done it once and for all, and to do it a second time would be tacitly to repudiate your own work. Afterward, whenever the memory of the offender or the offense happens to come into your mind, bless the delinquent briefly and dismiss the thought. Do this, however many times the thought may come back. After a few days it will return less and less often, until you forget it altogether. Then, perhaps after an interval, shorter or longer, the old trouble may come back to memory once more, but you will find that now all bitterness and resentment have disappeared, and you are both free with the perfect freedom of the children of God. Your forgiveness is complete. You will experience a wonderful joy in the realization of the demonstration.

Everybody should practice general forgiveness every day as a matter of course. When you say your daily prayers, issue a general amnesty, forgiving everyone who may have injured you in any way, and on no account particularize. Simply say: "I freely forgive everyone." Then in the course of the day, should the thought of grievance or resentment come up, bless the offender briefly and dismiss the thought.

The result of this policy will be that very soon you will find yourself cleared of all resentment and condemnation, and the effect upon your happiness, your bodily health, and your general life will be nothing less than revolutionary.

LEAD US NOT
INTO TEMPTATION
BUT DELIVER US
FROM EVIL

This clause has probably caused more difficulty than any other part of the Prayer. For many earnest people it has been a veritable stumbling block. They feel, and rightly, that God could not lead anyone into temptation or into evil in any circumstances, and so these words do not ring true.

For this reason, a number of attempts have been made to recast the wording. People have felt that Jesus could not have said what he is represented to have said, and so they look about for some phrasing which they think would be more in

accordance with the general tone of his teaching. Heroic efforts have been made to wrest the Greek original into something different. All this, however, is unnecessary. The Prayer
in the form in which we have it in English gives a perfectly
correct sense of the true inner meaning. Remember that
the Lord's Prayer covers the whole of the spiritual life. Condensed though the form is, it is nevertheless a complete manual for the development of the soul, and Jesus knew only too
well the subtle perils and difficulties that can and do beset
the soul when once the preliminary stages of spiritual unfoldment have been passed. Because those who are yet at a
comparatively early stage of development do not experience
such difficulties, they are apt to jump to the conclusion that
this clause is unnecessary; but such is not the case.

The facts are these—the more you pray, the more time
you spend in meditation and spiritual treatment, the more
sensitive you become. And if you spend a great deal of time
working on your soul in the right way, you will become
very sensitive. This is excellent; but like everything in the
universe, it works both ways. The more sensitive and spiritual you become, the more powerful and effective are your
prayers, you do better healing, and you advance rapidly. But,
for the same reason, you also become susceptible to forms
of temptation that simply do not beset those at an earlier
stage. You will also find that for ordinary faults, even things
that many men and women of the world would consider to

be trifling, you will be sharply punished, and this is well, because it keeps you up to the mark. The seemingly minor transgressions, the "little foxes that spoil the vines," would fritter away our spiritual power if not promptly dealt with.

No one at this level will be tempted to pick a pocket, or burgle a house; but this does not by any means imply that one will not have difficulties, and because of their subtlety, even greater difficulties to meet.

As we advance, new and powerful temptations await us on the path, ever ready to hurl us down if we are not watchful—temptations to work for self-glory, and self-aggrandizement instead of for God; for personal honors and distinctions, even for material gain; temptations to allow personal preferences to hold sway in our counsels when it is a sacred duty to deal with all men in perfect impartiality. Above and beyond all other sins the deadly sin of spiritual pride, truly "the last infirmity of noble mind," lurks on this road. Many fine souls who have triumphantly surmounted all other testings have lapsed into a condition of superiority and self-righteousness that has fallen like a curtain of steel between them and God. Great knowledge brings great responsibility. Great responsibility betrayed brings terrible punishment in its train. *Noblesse oblige* is preeminently true in spiritual things. One's knowledge of the Truth, however little it may be, is a sacred trust for humanity that must not be violated. While we should never make the mistake of casting our pearls before swine, nor urge the Truth in quarters where it is not welcome, yet we must do all that we wisely can to spread the true knowledge of God among mankind, that not one of "these little ones" may go hungry through our selfishness or our neglect. "Feed my lambs, feed my sheep."

The old occult writers were so vividly sensible of these dangers that, with their instinct for dramatization, they spoke of the soul as being challenged by various tests as it traversed the upward road. It was as though the traveler were halted at various gates or turnpike bars, and tested by some ordeal to determine whether he were ready to advance any further. If he succeeded in passing the test, they said, he was allowed to continue upon his way with the blessing of the challenger. If, however, he failed to survive the ordeal, he was forbidden to proceed.

Now, some less experienced souls, eager for rapid advancement, have rashly desired to be subjected immediately to all kinds of tests, and have even looked about, seeking for difficulties to overcome; as though one's own personality did not already present quite enough material for any one man or woman to deal with. Forgetting the lesson of our Lord's own ordeal in the wilderness, forgetting the injunction "Thou shalt not tempt the Lord thy God," they have virtually done this very thing, with sad results. And so Jesus has inserted this clause, in which we pray that we may not have to meet anything that is too much for us at the present level of our understanding. And, if we are wise, and work daily, as we should, for wisdom, understanding, purity, and the guidance of the Holy Spirit, we never shall find ourselves in any difficulty for which we have not the understanding necessary to clear ourselves. *Nothing shall by any means hurt you. Behold I am with you always.*

THINE IS THE KINGDOM AND THE POWER AND THE GLORY FOR EVER AND EVER

This is a wonderful gnomic saying summing up the essential truth of the Omnipresence and the All-ness of God. It means that God is indeed All in All, the doer, the doing, and the deed, and one can say also the spectator. The Kingdom in this sense means all creation, on every plane, for that is the Presence of God—God as manifestation or expression.

The Power, of course, is the Power of God. We know that God is the only power, and so, when we work, as when we pray, it is really God doing it by means of us. Just as the pianist produces his music by means of, or through his fingers, so may mankind be thought of as the fingers of God. His is the Power. If, when you are praying, you hold the thought that it is really God who is working through you, your prayers will gain immeasurably in efficiency. Say, "God is inspiring me." If, when you have any ordinary thing to do, you hold the thought, "Divine Intelligence is working through me now," you will perform the most difficult tasks with astonishing success.

The wondrous change that comes over us as we gradually realize what the Omnipresence of God really means, transfigures every phase of our lives, turning sorrow into joy, age into youth, and dullness into light and life. This is the glory—and the glory which comes to us is, of course, God's too. And the bliss we know in that experience is still God Himself, who is knowing that bliss through us.

In recent years, the Lord's Prayer has often been rewritten in the affirmative form. In this style, for instance, the clause "Thy kingdom come, thy will be done," becomes "Thy kingdom is come, thy will is being done." All such paraphrases are interesting and suggestive, but their importance is not vital. The affirmative form of prayer should be used for all healing work, but it is only one form of prayer. Jesus used the invocatory form very often, though not always, and the frequent use of this form is essential to the growth of the soul. It is not to be confused with supplicatory prayer, in which the subject begs and whines to God as a slave pleading with his master. That is always wrong. The highest of all forms of prayer is true contemplation, in which the thought and the thinker become one. This is the unity of the mystic, but it is rarely experienced in the earlier stages. Pray in whatever way you find easiest; for the easiest way is the best.

*Come unto me all ye that labor and are heavy laden and
I will give you rest.*

*The Lord is my light and my salvation; whom shall I
fear? The Lord is the strength of my life; of whom shall
I be afraid?*

*Though a host should encamp against me, my heart shall
not fear: though war should rise against me, in this
will I be confident.*

*When thou passest through the waters, I will be with
thee; and through the rivers, they shall not overflow
thee: when thou walkest through fire, thou shalt not
be burned; neither shall the flame kindle upon thee.*

As long as he sought the Lord, God made him to prosper.